A WAY OUT

A WAY OUT   Owen Fiss

America's Ghettos and the Legacy of Racism

EDITED BY JOSHUA COHEN, JEFFERSON DECKER, AND JOEL ROGERS

PRINCETON UNIVERSITY PRESS   *Princeton and Oxford*

Copyright © 2003 by Princeton University Press
Published by Princeton University Press, 41 William Street,
Princeton, New Jersey 08540
In the United Kingdom: Princeton University Press, 3 Market Place,
Woodstock, Oxfordshire OX20 1SY

Library of Congress Cataloging-in-Publication Data
Fiss, Owen M.
A way out : America's ghettos and the legacy of racism / Owen Fiss ; edited
by Joshua Cohen, Jefferson Decker, and Joel Rogers.
p. cm.
Includes bibliographical references and index.

ISBN: 0-691-08881-0

1. Social problems—United States. 2. Inner cities—Government policy—
United States. 3. Urban poor—Government policy—United States.
4. Occupational mobility—United States. I. Cohen, Joshua, 1951–
II. Decker, Jefferson. III. Rogers, Joel, 1952– IV. Title.

HN59.2 .F574 2003
361.1'0973—dc21   2002030718

British Library Cataloging-in-Publication Data is available

This book has been composed in Adobe Caslon and Futura

Printed on acid-free paper. ∞

www.pupress.princeton.edu

Printed in the United States of America

1 3 5 7 9 10 8 6 4 2

TO BURKE MARSHALL

a tribute to all that is good and decent in the law

CONTENTS

PREFACE

Joshua Cohen, Jefferson Decker, and Joel Rogers

▓ The United States, Lincoln said, is dedicated to the proposition that all men are created equal. That founding ideal has never been fully realized, but the distance between promise and performance is nowhere more evident than in America's inner cities. In this book, Owen Fiss, one of the country's leading constitutional theorists, offers some innovative ideas about how to close this great gap.

America's ghettos, Fiss argues, are systems of social subordination that substantially result from government policy, and not simply products of unfortunate life choices or bad luck. Because the state is not an innocent bystander, it has an obligation to correct these violations of fundamental constitutional principles. Moreover, the social problems in American ghettos—high unemployment, poor schools, crime, drugs, and weak secondary institutions—are self-reinforcing. So we cannot expect to be able to correct the troubles on site. Fiss concludes that the state has an obligation to help residents move from ghettos to communities where they are more likely to find jobs, reasonable schools, and the other rudiments of a decent life. Such a policy would, of course, be very expensive: Fiss estimates the near-term costs at $50 billion a year. Moreover, the social disruption could be very great. But justice, Fiss argues, demands no less.

Fiss's respondents are less sure about the proposed remedy. Though several agree that mobility is part of the solution, two considerations qualify the agreement. The first is that Fiss underestimates the internal resources in inner-city communities and exaggerates the virtues of the communities into which residents would be expected to move. The second is about political will. Observing current skepticism about ambitious public policy, the persistence of racism, and the likely resistance of receiving communities, several respondents conclude that resources might be better invested in inner cities themselves. What is not at all in dispute is the persistent failure to deliver on this country's founding promise. On this, Fiss speaks for all: We need affirmative political remedies "to dismantle . . . the caste structure that has disfigured our nation from the very beginning."

PART I

WHAT SHOULD BE DONE FOR THOSE WHO HAVE BEEN LEFT BEHIND?

OWEN FISS

There is so much to celebrate in America. The nation is the strongest and most prosperous the world has ever known. We have enjoyed the blessings of a constitutional democracy for more than two hundred years. Civil society is endowed with effective and vibrant private institutions. The United States economy is highly productive and is the locomotive that drives the world economy. With a remarkably high standard of living, we are imbued with the sense of power and satisfaction that comes from having so many of the things that money can buy—travel, leisure, cars, and beautiful homes.

In the shadow of this glory, profound problems persist, some close to the core of our civilization. Perhaps the most glaring is the presence in our cities of communities known as ghettos. The persons living in the typical ghetto are black, but, even more significant, they are poor. Many are on welfare, and even those who work tend to earn amounts that place them beneath the poverty line. As a consequence, the housing stock is old and dilapidated, retail establishments scarce, crime rates high, gangs rampant, drugs plentiful, and jobs in short supply.

Living under such adverse conditions tests the human spirit. It demands resiliency and ingenuity, and a fair measure of faith. The survivors are often strong and determined individuals, who, through hard work and the elemental bonds of love and friendship, have made a life in the inner city for themselves and their families. The ghetto is their home. It has also been home for some of America's most talented writers and artists. Yet alongside these individual truths is a collective one, vividly and poignantly described by James Baldwin forty years ago in *Letter from a Region in My Mind*. The ghettos of America were produced by the most blatant racial exclusionary practices. As a vestige of our unique and unfortunate racial history, they continue to isolate and concentrate the most disadvantaged and, through this very isolation and concentration, perpetuate and magnify that disadvantage.

Since the time that Baldwin wrote and during the Second Reconstruction—the period in American history begun by *Brown v. Board of Education*—some black families have managed to flee the confines of the ghetto, as Baldwin and the most gifted of his generation once did. These families now live in more upscale neighborhoods, a few integrated, the others predominantly black. The poor and jobless have remained behind in the ghetto, their numbers swollen and their plight worsened as both jobs and those who succeeded economically left the inner city. Housing stock aged, social institutions deteriorated, and crime escalated. By concentrating and isolating the poor and jobless, the ghetto turned neighbors on each other and, over time, created a sector of the black community known as the underclass. The members of this class suffer from a multitude of disadvantages that can ultimately be traced to racial discrimination and its economic consequences. Those disadvantages prevent them from enjoying the splendor of America or improving their position. They are the worst off in our society, and their plight stands as an affront to the ideal of equality embodied in the Fourteenth Amendment.

Many strategies have been devised for addressing the needs of the underclass, some even tried. All are imperfect. The disparity between the magnitude of the problems and the modesty of the proposed remedies is simply overwhelming. The most tempting are those that leave the ghetto intact while attempting to improve the day-to-day life of those who remain confined there. Examples of such remedies include creating jobs, allocating new resources to local schools, and strengthening the enforcement of the criminal laws. What all these remedies overlook, however, is that the ghetto itself is a structure of subordination, which, by isolating and concentrating the most disadvantaged, creates the very dynamics that render the quality of life of those forced to live in it so miserable and their prospect for success so bleak.

The only strategy with any meaningful chance of success is one that ends the ghetto as a feature of American life. Pursuing this remedy requires providing those who are trapped in the ghetto with the economic resources necessary to move to better neighborhoods—black or white—if they so choose. With the means to move, most will leave, and that will be enough to break the concentration of mutually reinforcing destructive forces—poverty, joblessness, crime, poorly functioning social institutions—that turn the ghetto into a structure of subordination. The physical space that once belonged to the ghetto quickly will be reclaimed by developers and transformed into a new, up-and-coming neighborhood.

Providing ghetto residents with such a choice of residence in a way that promotes economic integration has been tried with success in the very recent past, though only through pilot programs with very limited reach. I believe that we must expand these programs and defend them on the grounds of justice. The ghetto is responsible for the creation and maintenance of the black underclass, and the proposed deconcentration program should be seen as a remedy for the role that society and its agent, the state, have played in constructing the ghetto in the first place.

Providing the resources necessary for such a program will have vast economic consequences for the country. Great human and social costs will also be involved. Means might be devised to facilitate moving and to lessen the disruption of a move. But no matter what, those who take advantage of the opportunity to leave will lose the comfort and support of neighbors they have known over the years and will face substantial hardships in adjusting to new communities. Because many are likely to leave, those who consider staying put will find the context of their decision radically altered. Communities will be broken up, and receiving communities will need to undergo long processes of adjustment.

All these consequences, like the conflicts engendered by earlier efforts at school desegregation, are very disturbing. Yet they seem inescapable. The only alternative to a program that seeks to expand choice is to condemn a sector of the black community to suffer in perpetuity from the devastating effects of our racial history.

THE PROBLEM

Although our ghettos were never surrounded by the physical walls that often marked the European ones, a blend of economics and racial practices produced the same sense of confinement.

Over the course of the twentieth century, principally starting after the First World War, millions of blacks left the agricultural areas of the South and moved to the growing urban centers of the nation, some in the South, others in the North and West. These migrants had no savings and few employable skills. The skills they acquired on the farms and plantations were of very limited value in the cities, and the poor education they had earlier received only compounded their competitive disadvantage. Most were educated under the Jim Crow system and thus attended schools that were systematically short-changed and grossly inferior. Separate schools were never equal.

The newcomers settled in urban sectors with the oldest and poorest housing stock, and remained clustered in these neighborhoods. Initially this form of segregation might have been attributable to the very understandable desire, shared by every group of immigrants, to seek the help and support of friends and relatives. But more pernicious dynamics were also at work, which excluded the black migrants from white neighborhoods and endowed their segregation with a remarkable degree of permanence.

Even in the North, the newcomers encountered Jim Crow, though often in new guise. Children were nominally assigned to schools on the basis of residence, but the segregation of neighborhoods and the gerrymandering of attendance zones insured that blacks attended one set of schools and whites another. The education blacks received was, once again, inferior and provided them with few of the skills necessary for upward mobility. Their parents and others of working age were either barred from employment or relegated to the lowest-paying or most-demeaning jobs because of race.

As a result, it was almost impossible for the newcomers to the cities to improve their economic position or even to imagine a move to a better neighborhood. In the years following the Second World War, the federal government responded to the needs of the very poor by building housing projects. Although rent was subsidized, the construction of public housing only reinforced racial housing patterns. Local authorities, knowing that the occupants were likely to be black, confined these projects to the black areas of the city.

Even the few blacks who prospered economically or professionally found it difficult, if not impossible, to rent an apartment or buy a house in a white neighborhood. At one point in our history, the municipal zoning power was used explicitly to confine blacks to certain areas of the city. After such ordinances were declared illegal in 1917, greater reliance was placed on racially restrictive covenants, which obliged buyers never to sell their newly acquired houses to blacks. In 1948 the Supreme Court declared racial covenants illegal, but other barriers persisted.

White property owners refused to sell or rent to blacks. Some banks refused to make home mortgage loans to blacks altogether, and others disfavored so-called changing neighborhoods. Those blacks who were lucky enough to find a willing seller or landlord and dared to move to a white neighborhood faced great hostility and harassment, sometimes even violence. Lorraine Hansberry's *A Raisin in the Sun*, which opened on Broadway in 1959 and two years later was released as a film, still stands as a monument to the ordeal of a black family moving to a white neighborhood.

Usually the state acquiesced in these exclusionary practices. Sometimes it actively supported them, even after the Supreme Court declared racially restrictive zoning and covenants to be illegal. In the postwar era, the Federal Housing Administration (FHA) played a pivotal role in the development of the suburbs by issuing home mortgages and lowering the cost of housing. As Kenneth Jackson explains in *Crabgrass Frontier* (1985), the FHA consistently promoted, or at least reinforced, bank practices that made it virtually impossible for blacks to get mortgages for homes in white neighborhoods. The FHA *Underwriting Manual* in force during the 1950s warned that "if a neighborhood is to retain stability, it is necessary that properties shall continue to be occupied by the same social and racial classes."

In time these policies were also abandoned, but others were instituted that had similar effects. As late as 1964 the voters of California approved an initiative, the notorious Proposition 14, that reaffirmed the right of property owners to sell or rent to whomever they wished. This measure was described by the Supreme Court as a thinly veiled attempt to encourage racial discrimination. It was held unconstitutional in 1967.

In April 1968, in the immediate wake of the assassination of Martin Luther King Jr., Congress passed a federal fair housing law. The law created new opportunities for those who had the economic means to move out of the ghettos into more affluent, typically white neighborhoods. Admittedly blacks seeking to move had to cope with resistance to that law and considerable hostility. Still, the 1968 law made exodus from the ghettos easier and thus began to chip away at one important source of confinement.

When the fair housing act was initially passed, only a few blacks were able, as a practical matter, to take advantage of their newly expanded freedom. Yet over the next thirty years this changed. The number of blacks financially able to leave the ghettos increased significantly, thanks to the general growth of the economy and, perhaps even more important, to a number of civil rights strategies instituted during the Second Reconstruction.

During this period, efforts were made to spread resources more equitably among schools and to give black Americans access to some of the better elementary and secondary schools. The 1954 decision of the Supreme Court in *Brown v. Board of Education* decreed as much, but it was not until the late 1960s that open resistance to that decision was overcome and practical steps, usually under court order or threat of terminating federal financial assistance, were taken to implement it. In lock-step fashion, the doors of higher education were also opened to blacks.

A federal fair employment law was enacted in 1964, and full enforcement began in 1968. Affirmative action programs also appeared in the late 1960s and early 1970s, and over the next thirty years dramatically enhanced the process of integration. These programs gave preferential treatment to blacks in employment and in certain educational sectors that controlled access to the professions and other high-paying careers.

As a result of all these policies, plus a growing economy, a sector of the black community—generally referred to as the black middle class—emerged with the economic means to exercise the freedom conferred under the 1968 fair housing law. These individuals claimed for themselves what has long been thought part of the American dream—moving to a better neighborhood. It is hard to leave friends and familiar surroundings, but everyone recognizes that the quality of life—vulnerability to crime, the nature of one's kids' friends and classmates, the quality of stores and housing—depends, in good part, on one's neighborhood. Many people move when they have the economic means to do so, and the new black middle class was no exception. Most moved to what were then white, middle-class neighborhoods. Some of these stabilized as racially integrated neighborhoods; others experienced so-called white flight and emerged as middle-class black neighborhoods.

Like Baldwin and the lucky few of his generation, the families who moved during this period were the exception. Against all odds, they were able to seize the new opportunities created during the Second Reconstruction and escape the harsh realities of ghetto life. But the bulk of those living in the ghetto remained there, bearing the full burden of America's racial history, stymied by poverty and by the discriminatory practices that persist to this very day in housing, employment, and education. Indeed, ghettos have continued to grow in recent decades, both in geographical reach and population. In 1970, 2.4 million blacks lived in neighborhoods where more than 40 percent of the persons were below the official poverty line. By 1990 the number had risen to 4.2 million. The comparable figure from the 2000 census is not yet available, but it is fair to assume that the same trajectory has continued. During the boom of the 1990s the poverty rate among blacks declined modestly. During the same period, however, the economic position of some sectors of the black community deteriorated, the birth rate remained high, and the pronounced degree of residential segregation that characterized most of America's cities persisted.

Although moving out of the ghetto presumably improved the quality of life of those who moved, it had an unfortunate effect on the economic and social profile of the community they left. It turned the black ghetto into a community of the most disadvantaged. It enhanced the isolation and concentration of the poor, weakened social institutions, and distanced the community from those with the greatest economic and social resources, many of whom were also valuable role models. Surely some people remained because they valued their established relationships above all else; others may have remained for religious or political reasons and continued to exercise leadership in the community. My own sense, however, is that they, too, were the exception and that most of those who stayed did so because they had little choice.

As the black middle class left the ghetto, jobs also began to disappear. Some plants once located in the inner city fell to global competition and closed. Others moved to suburban communities to take advantage of cheaper land, proximity to highways and airports, lower crime rates, and perhaps a workforce that appeared to be better educated or more able. Racial assumptions about the ability of the workforce undoubtedly played some role in these calculations, but the economic logic was also manifest. Overall the result was devastating. Jobs left the community at the same time as the most successful left, worsening the plight of those remaining behind.

Like the propensity of the upwardly mobile to move to better neighborhoods, commuting to work is a familiar American tradition. The hour commute from Stamford, Connecticut, to New York's financial district is not at all unusual. Those who remained in the ghetto were not, however, readily able to adapt to the relocation of jobs by this means, and commuting from the inner city to the suburbs was difficult, in some cases impossible. The distances were long, the pay for the jobs available was insufficient to cover the costs of whatever transportation might exist, and working outside one's immediate neighborhood was especially difficult for parents of small children, who wanted to be available for calls from schools and day care providers.

Ghetto residents also faced a mismatch of skills. In one important respect, the economic plight of inner-city neighborhoods parallels a broader trend in the United States over the last thirty years—the decline of manufacturing jobs. For America, in general, the void has been filled by a growing service sector, which takes the Stamford commuter to Manhattan. But most of these new jobs were unavailable to those left behind in the ghetto, who, inevitably, had the lowest educational achievements and little work experience. They were not in a position to compete for high-paying jobs in finance or communications. True, entry-level jobs in retail establishments, hotels, and other service providers remained within reach, but few such jobs existed in their immediate neighborhoods because the residents were poor. One study reported that the ratio of applicants to those recently hired at fast-food restaurants in Harlem was fourteen-to-one.

We thus confront the fact that over the last thirty years—just as the black middle class has left the ghettos—joblessness in those communities has risen. In the 1980s William Julius Wilson called attention to the emergence of the black middle class and how different their situation was compared to that of ghetto residents. In 1996 Wilson opened his new book, *When Work Disappears*, with this startling observation: "For the first time in the twentieth century most adults in many inner-city ghetto neighborhoods are not working in a typical week." To be sure, many of these adults have child care responsibilities, unmistakably work, but which Wilson excluded from his calculus. Also, those who cannot work because of age or disability need to be taken into account. Still, the fact that a very large percentage of the adults in certain urban neighborhoods are jobless is astonishing. It well warrants the stir that Wilson's book caused.

At the very least, joblessness means no income. It produces poverty and leads to dependence on the welfare system, with all the stigmatization and loss of self-esteem such dependence entails. The impact of joblessness goes even deeper. Drawing on the work of Pierre Bourdieu and, before it, the famed study of Marienthal by Marie Jahoda, Paul Lazarsfeld, and Hans Zeisel, Wilson explained how joblessness deprives people of the patterned set of expectations that teaches discipline, instills our activities with meaning, and provides a framework for daily life. Individuals without jobs are not only poor; their sense of self-efficacy weakens, and they are less able to cope with life's challenges. They are also probably bored. Sustained joblessness can lead to activities that are self-destructive and a threat to others, most often neighbors. It might lead individuals to seek such palliatives as drugs and alcohol; or it might lead them to join gangs, which import a structure to ordinary life but pursue antisocial ends.

The concentration of the jobless and poor in one relatively compact geographic area intensifies both the deprivation and barriers to upward mobility. So does the weakening of social institutions and networks that results from the exodus of those who made it. The community is left to turn on itself, exposing those in the ghetto to a heightened risk of crime and violence, which degrades the quality of life in the community and creates further incentives for individual families and local businesses to flee. The sense of isolation increases as the quality of life spirals downward.

In the course of this process, community norms and expectations also change. Wilson explains how criminal activity or long-term welfare dependency often become adaptive strategies for those living within the confines of the ghetto. Eventually these activities become normalized and are perceived as legitimate by significant sectors of the community. This change in attitude and expectations increases the prevalence of activities so destructive of self and others—what Wilson politely calls "ghetto-related behavior." These activities magnify the deprivations of those living within the ghetto and further foreclose the possibility of upward economic mobility for both the individuals engaged in them and the community at large.

In these ways the ghetto has become, even more so than when Baldwin first wrote, a structure of subordination. More than a sum of individual disadvantages, the ghetto is the mechanism through which we have created and maintained the black underclass, a group saddled with a multitude of burdens— above all, joblessness and poverty—that relegates its members to the lowest stratum in society and locks them into it.

SOCIAL RESOURCES

A community is more than a collection of individuals. It is also made up of institutions—from the family to churches to schools—that give it coherence and identity, and sustain those who live there. These social resources are available in the ghetto, of course, but they have been adversely affected by the same dynamics, above all joblessness and the legacy of discrimination, that have transformed the ghetto into a community of the worst off and compounded its isolation. The institutions of the ghetto are unable to counter the downward spiral in the quality of life of those who live there and, in fact, may work to entrench the underclass even more deeply.

The family's capacity to perform ordinary social functions in the ghetto is limited by the prevalence there of single-parent families. Although recent decades have witnessed higher rates of single parenthood throughout the nation, the trend in the ghetto is exceptional. More than 70 percent of black households residing in extreme poverty are headed by single women. Even more striking is the number of such women who became mothers in their teenage years. Recent statistics indicate a drop in the rate of teen births, but the numbers remain disturbing. In 1990, 6 percent of all teenage women throughout the nation became mothers; in 1997, the number was 5.2 percent.

The challenge facing teenage mothers is staggering, particularly in the ghetto. Barely able to fend for themselves, they are called on to protect their children, instill in them socially constructive values, teach them social skills, and help them to develop goals and aspirations. No wonder, as Orlando Patterson reports in *The Ordeal of Integration* (1997), that when the children of teenage mothers become teenagers themselves they are less likely to finish school, three times more likely to be incarcerated, and significantly more likely to become teenage mothers themselves.

People often turn outside the immediate family for help in raising children. Sometimes the surrogate parent is a grandparent, uncle, or aunt; often it is a neighbor. But, in the ghetto, the problems of the immediate family—sustained joblessness or the presence of only a single parent, sometimes a teenager—are often replicated in the extended family and larger community. Sometimes these problems are compounded by the scars of the most blatant forms of racism. A grandfather who has been without meaningful work for decades is not likely to be an ideal care provider, let alone a role model, for the child of his sixteen-year-old granddaughter. An aunt who was herself an unmarried mother at age fifteen, and who has spent the last decade in a state of dependency, may not be an ideal surrogate parent for her newborn nephew. Nor are the immediate neighbors, many of whom are—in part thanks to the exodus of the black middle class—poor, jobless, or young single parents themselves.

Some families may turn for help to local churches, which have long been important institutions in the black community and were once the source of many leaders of the civil rights movement. Today that movement has lost much of its steam, but black ministers continue to act as spokespersons for the black community and as persons capable of organizing and activating that community. In that respect, the work of Eugene Rivers and his colleagues in Boston, who have served as buffers between the police and the citizens of Dorchester and Roxbury, is exemplary. Yet it remains doubtful that the church can take the place of the family and supply discipline and structure to children who lack direction. This is not to deny the sometimes heroic achievements of a number of black ministers, but only to recognize the limited capacity of the black church to counter the ghetto's many destructive dynamics, day in and day out.

Many black churches do not even serve the ghetto. Some are located in middle-class black neighborhoods and minister to the needs of those communities. Others are geographically situated in the ghetto but draw their members from families who once lived there but now reside in the suburbs or upper- or middle-class communities. The trip on Sunday mornings to the old neighborhood may provoke powerful memories, but over time these memories fade, and the ghetto and its distinctive

needs become more distant. Even those churches that are located in the ghetto and draw their membership from the neighborhood cannot fully compensate for the limits of the local
family as a socializing institution nor combat the destructive
dynamics of the ghetto.

The power of these churches to serve the community in this
way may be limited by the increasing secularization of American culture, which is as prevalent in the ghettos as in the cities
of which they are a part. A few years ago William Finnegan
published an extraordinary and now rightly famous portrait of a
young man involved in drug trafficking in New Haven's ghetto.
Entitled *Out There*, Finnegan's essay described this young
man's family situation and social network in some detail, and
made clear that neither he nor his friends had any ties to the
local churches. They were as fully secularized as most New
Haven teenagers, though, of course, they confronted a different
predicament—how to participate in the riches of our consumer
culture with little or no income from lawful employment.

James Baldwin, writing from his own experiences in Harlem
in the 1950s, fully understood the appeal in the ghetto of the
evangelical churches and the Nation of Islam. They seemed to
promise to the young not just salvation but also the structure,
discipline, and coherence absent in many ghetto families. Yet
the capacity of these organizations to deliver on this promise
has always been limited by the reluctance of parents to cede
control of their children to another institution. Baldwin joined
the church at age fourteen but only over his father's strong ob-
jection. Account must also be taken of the possibility that certain less constructive characteristics of ghetto life might be replicated in the local churches—which, to some extent, reflect the

culture of the neighborhood of which they are a part. They are likely to be as poor and as needy as their parishioners.

Access to other intermediate organizations is not controlled by parents, and, accordingly, these organizations might have greater potential than churches to serve as parents' surrogates. But because they, too, are neighborhood-based and thus largely populated by youngsters who grow up with insufficient family support or control, they can hardly fill the void. Local gangs teach discipline but most often in the service of criminal ends. Public schools stand ready to socialize the children entrusted to their care by law, but schools are encumbered because enrollment is normally determined on the basis of residence. Thus elementary and secondary schools in a ghetto contain a heavy concentration of children who come from families wracked by joblessness and poverty, headed often by a single, very young parent.

A student body drawn from such families places an enormous burden on the teacher, often making ghetto schools the least preferred among teachers who have a choice. In addition, a high concentration of very poor children impairs that portion of the learning process that comes from one's classmates. In *All Together Now: Creating Middle Class Schools Through Public Choice* (2001), Richard D. Kahlenberg refers to this aspect of the learning process as the "hidden curriculum" and explains how it works: "In high poverty schools, peers are likely to have smaller vocabularies and less knowledge to share; they tend to have lower aspirations and negative attitudes toward achievement and to engage in anti-achievement behavior (cutting classes, failing to do homework)." Kahlenberg also describes the dynamics that keep parents of these children from fully involving themselves in school activities and from pressuring the authorities to make sure that these schools are staffed by the very best teachers available.

As a result of these dynamics, ghetto schools are likely to fail, not just in fulfilling their academic mission—teaching cognitive skills and knowledge of the world—but also in their less well-defined socialization function: imposing discipline, building confidence, heightening aspirations, and instilling the values needed for personal success and a well-functioning society. Public schools in other communities are important instruments of social mobility, but not those in the typical urban ghetto. The challenge they confront is overwhelming. Kenneth B. Clark described this challenge in his 1965 book, *Dark Ghetto*. He warned that the public schools of the ghettos "are becoming an instrument for the perpetuation—and strengthening—of class and caste, while the elite cluster in their safe suburban schools or in the exclusive private schools." Contemporary realities confirm his fears.

THE FAILURE OF FAMILIAR REMEDIES

A wide variety of public remedies have been proposed to deal with the plight of the underclass, and with the limited capacity of families, churches, schools, and other institutions in the community to address the dynamics of deprivation. Understandably, government has tended to favor those remedies that preserve urban neighborhoods and that focus on isolated features of these dynamics.

The 1996 federal welfare reform act can be understood in such terms. Imposing a five-year limit on the receipt of welfare over a life time, the statute was designed to create incentives or pressure for welfare recipients to find work. This measure implicitly recognized the destructive impact of joblessness and the importance of work—even low-paid work—for the self-esteem it engenders and the structure it gives to daily existence. The fear was also present that the availability of welfare without any time limits might encourage women to have children regardless of their economic ability to provide for them. In fact, the 1996 welfare reform measure was often presented as a strategy to combat teenage pregnancy and the rise of single-parent families.

Before the enactment of the 1996 measure, a number of states instituted experimental programs intended to move individuals from welfare rolls to the workforce. Based on a comprehensive review of the evidence, Robert Solow reports in *Work and Welfare* (1998) that moving people from welfare to work was much harder than lawmakers had anticipated. None of the more than a dozen welfare-to-work programs he reviewed, Solow writes, "offers grounds for optimism about the ability of welfare recipients to find and hold jobs, or to earn a decent living." Without additional supports, he concludes, "the transformation of welfare into work is likely to be the transformation of welfare into unemployment and casual earnings so low as once to have been thought unacceptable for fellow citizens."

The 1996 reform extended these experimental programs to the nation at large, but without the additional supports that Solow urged. Although they were given the freedom to determine which families were eligible for assistance, the states faced fiscal penalties unless a certain percentage of families were working or engaged in work-related activities such as searching for a job. On top of this, the states were prohibited from using federal funds for providing assistance to any family for more than five years.

Following the enactment, the welfare rolls dropped dramatically—by almost 60 percent. Many attributed this development to the new law, but the economic boom may have had at least as much to do with it. During the 1990s unemployment reached historic new lows, below 5 percent. With the end of the boom and unemployment edging back up in 2001 and 2002, thousands of families will reach the five-year limit imposed by the 1996 law just as the demand for employees decreases. It is not at all clear where poor families will turn for support.

Nor should the effectiveness of the 1996 reform be measured solely in terms of the decrease in the welfare rolls. A 2002 study reported that 40 percent of the families who left welfare are not working, and many of those who are working find themselves in low-paying, dead-end jobs with no benefits. They can barely scrape by. The bulk of welfare recipients are single mothers, and although the 1996 law pressures them to get out of the house and look for work, it does not require states to make adequate provision for child care services. One can only wonder what will happen to the children of those who somehow manage to find a job. Under the best circumstances the 1996 reform may reduce welfare dependency and many of the dysfunctions allegedly associated with it, but only by putting the welfare of children at jeopardy and thereby entrenching the underclass across generations.

Tougher and more aggressive police tactics—to end, what some consider, the underenforcement of the criminal law in the ghetto—entail a similar danger. The hope is that by reducing criminal activity in the inner city, we will curtail the victimization of those who live there and, at the same time, reduce the exodus of jobs and people from the community. It is doubtful that these

new police tactics—for example, blanket searches of public housing projects in pursuit of illegal arms—will have any immediate
impact on crime rates. More fundamentally, we need to consider
the impact of these tactics on the life of the community. The
level of crime may be reduced, but only at the cost of ushering
in an oppressive police regime. Such a regime is of concern to
everyone, particularly to ghetto residents who remember all too
well abuses at the hands of the police. Recent experiences will
refresh the memory of those who may have forgotten.

Others sought to deal with the high level of criminal activity in the ghetto by enhancing sentences for drug-related
crimes. They have declared a War on Drugs. Over time, this
war may deter some criminal activity, but only by increasing
the number of young males from the ghetto who will spend a
good portion of their lives in prison. This would impoverish
the ghetto community further by reducing its available labor
force and would exacerbate the dynamics that already produce
so many single-parent families. Those eventually released will
confront the same obstacles that every ex-con faces in finding
a well-paying job.

Other government interventions may have greater short-run
chances of success. One is Head Start, which has its roots in
the civil rights era and, more specifically, in the War on Poverty.
Recognizing that the family is sometimes an inadequate socializing institution, Head Start, a preschool program for three-
and four-year olds, reaches children at an early age and lasts
for a year or two. Although all children from poor families are
eligible, most Head Start programs are based in the ghetto. As
is true for the standard elementary and secondary schools in
the ghettos, the burden these programs take on is immense,

given their neighborhood-centered quality and the backgrounds of the children they receive.

Head Start can succeed only through enormous investments. In 2001 the annual federal appropriation for Head Start was around $6.2 billion, but this figure significantly understates the needs that Head Start is designed to address. Presently Head Start serves only about one-third of the estimated number of children eligible, with most enrolled in part-day programs that last only eight months. Because there are some fifteen hundred grantees, comprising more than eighteen thousand local learning centers, the standards of Head Start programs vary throughout the country. Showcase federally funded preschool projects, such as the Perry Preschool Project in Ypsilanti, Michigan, and the Carolina Abcedarian Project in Chapel Hill, North Carolina, where the greatest achievements have been observed, were not Head Start programs and, in fact, were funded at per-child rates of almost double the national average for Head Start.

But even if funding were increased, as indeed it should be, Head Start would be a radically incomplete response to the everyday needs young children encounter growing up in what William Julius Wilson terms, in an effort to be realistic about the prospects of any preschool program, "the harsh environment of the inner-city ghetto." Head Start is only a beginning, but, even so, we can expect the lessons Head Start teaches to be unlearned once the child reaches a certain age, leaves the program, enters a public school, and suffers the full force of that environment. The benefits of Head Start will soon fade. Indeed, well-documented studies indicate that initial improvements in test scores among Head Start participants tend to recede by the time an average child reaches the third grade. Even more disturbing, the fade-out effect differs across populations, occurring more quickly among blacks. This, of course, is not at all surprising given the conditions of life on the ghetto street and the quality of education available in the local public schools, where resources, student/teacher ratios, and the length of the school day and year are likely to be set on a citywide basis, without consideration of the special needs of inner-city communities. (Janet Currie and Duncan Thomas present their findings on these issues in the 1995 *American Economic Review* and again in the 2000 *Journal of Human Resources*.) Programs such as Head Start will make a difference in the lives of a few—who are likely to exit the ghetto—and for that reason must be continued and their funding strengthened as long as the ghetto exists. But they will not have a broad enough impact to break the ghetto's overall confining grip.

Perhaps the most promising remedies are those that seek to deal with the spatial mismatch between workers and jobs: the fact that jobs have moved to the suburbs while potential workers remain in the inner city. One strategy—the creation of enterprise zones in the inner city—provides economic incentives for businesses to relocate or simply to remain there. Such incentives have to compensate for higher land costs, increased security needs, and perhaps even lower skill levels in the ghetto workforce because of sustained joblessness and inadequate social institutions. The economic logic behind the move of businesses to the suburbs seems so compelling, however, that there is reason to doubt the efficacy of such programs.

Empirical studies support such skepticism about the effectiveness of enterprise zones. They also explain why these measures have fallen out of fashion. After reviewing studies of a dozen enterprise zone initiatives, Rebecca Blank concludes in her 1997 book, *It Takes a Nation*, that such programs generate few new jobs and that those that are created pay poorly and come at an exorbitant financial cost. Paul Jargowsky is also critical of these programs. As he explains in *Poverty and Place* (1997), because enterprise zones fail to address the larger, metropolitan-level dynamics responsible for inner-city joblessness, they can never incorporate severely deprived neighborhoods "into the mainstream economy but will only sustain them at a minimal level with a patchwork of subsidies and handouts."

William Julius Wilson, also concerned with the spatial mismatch, fully understands the difficulties of bringing business back to the ghetto and, as a result has thrown his support behind still another strategy for bringing jobs there: a neo-Works Progress Administration (WPA) program. The government would hire the unemployed, much as it did during the New Deal, to do jobs that improve the quality of life in the ghetto. These workers could repair the streets, clean the parks, construct new playgrounds, and perhaps even run various social programs.

Like enterprise zones, Wilson's proposal does not have much chance of working. Certainly, the government can create jobs and open them to everyone, but what sorts of jobs will they be? How much will they pay? And what will be the chances of advancement? In essence, Wilson responds to these worries in a single, succinct sentence: "Most workers in the inner city are ready, willing, able, and anxious to hold a steady job." Notice that Wilson refers to "workers," not the "jobless," who, he told us, were the norm in the ghetto, and he fails to give any specific content to the phrase "steady job." In truth, Wilson's rejoinder is at odds with the governing sociological insight of his book:

that sustained joblessness not only produces poverty but also undermines character. Joblessness removes structure from individuals' lives and tends to cause people to be decidedly not "willing, able, and anxious" to take the government jobs Wilson envisions.

Although a large number of ghetto residents may have flocked to the new McDonald's in search of work, they are unlikely to pursue Wilson's neo-WPA jobs with great intensity. Such jobs contain few opportunities for advancement and would be tinged with the stigma our society associates with any government handout. They are likely to be viewed as make-work. Wilson contemplates that the wages of the new government jobs would be slightly below minimum wage, but even if they were above the minimum they would be very low, certainly not a living wage. Another welfare program—say, an expanded Earned Income Tax Credit—would be needed to lift these employees above the official poverty line.

More fundamentally, Wilson's proposal, or, for that matter, any program to end the spatial mismatch by bringing jobs to the ghetto, slights the structural dimension of the problem—specifically, that the jobless individual is situated in a neighborhood with lots of other jobless individuals and that over the years this neighborhood has been wracked by a host of destructive forces. Job creation in the ghetto must not only overcome the reluctance of any particular individual to accept a menial job but must also reckon with this individual's membership in a community or group of similarly situated individuals. Together, these individuals exert pressure on one another and produce a culture in the ghetto that makes it most unlikely that a job creation program such as the one Wilson proposes will work.

AN ALTERNATIVE

Any ameliorative strategy must confront the fact that the ghetto is more than a place where the underclass happens to live. It is a social structure that concentrates and isolates the most disadvantaged and creates its own distinctive culture, and thus is integral to the perpetuation of the underclass. It is the paramount mechanism through which a historically subordinated group continues to be kept far beneath others in terms of wealth, power, and living standards. Accordingly, we need strategies that promise to dismantle that structure—to tear down the walls of the ghetto. To speak less metaphorically, we must provide those who still are trapped in the ghetto with the economic means to move into middle- or upper-class neighborhoods.

Such a voluntary relocation strategy would eliminate the spatial mismatch between jobs and residence by allowing the jobless to move closer to the jobs. It would break up the concentration of impoverished, single-parent households by enabling ghetto residents to move to safer neighborhoods where there is a greater mix of economic classes and family structures. It would also enhance access to schools, churches, and other intermediate institutions that are not so heavily burdened as those of the ghetto and that are more likely to facilitate social mobility.

This strategy would improve the lives of the adults who choose to move by situating them in communities where jobs exist, and thus enable them to transform their lives into something more fulfilling and productive. It would also break the entrenchment of the underclass across generations because children in families that relocated would reap the benefits of

safer, more positive surroundings and greater institutional resources. Of course, middle- and upper-class neighborhoods,
both black and white, have their own dysfunctions. Still, they
have advantages over the ghetto in terms of safety, social services, education, and employment opportunities. Moving to
those neighborhoods would capitalize on those advantages.

The strategic advantage of choosing racially integrated or predominantly white middle- and upper-class neighborhoods as receiving communities should not be overlooked. Tying the fate
of blacks to that of whites in this way may be the most reliable
means of securing equal protection for the minority because it
guarantees that every gain enjoyed by whites in social services
or neighborhood improvements will redound to the benefit of
blacks. The integrative ideal affirmed by *Brown v. Board of Education* rested, in part, on the fear that the majority would always
shortchange the schools attended only by the minority.

Although such gains might be achieved if families relocated
to racially integrated or predominantly white middle- and
upper-class neighborhoods, the receiving communities need be
defined only by class. Because the concentration of the poor
and jobless functions as the engine of subordination, economic
integration must be the centerpiece of any suitable remedy. A
black middle-class community created over the last thirty years
as a result of antidiscrimination laws in housing and employment would thus be a suitable receiving community for residents moving from the ghetto, as would an upscale racially integrated or predominantly white community. Sometimes the
search for such neighborhoods might take us beyond the city
limits, sometimes not. In either case, the move will mean enhanced access to jobs, better schools and social services, nicer
housing, and higher-quality retail establishments.

Those who decide to move must not, however, be regrouped into another ghetto. The ghetto is a structure of subordination, and the purpose of this program is to enable people to leave it. So care must be taken not simply to move from one site to another a concentration of poor, jobless, single-parent families headed by teenagers. To achieve this objective, an agency needs to be created that would seek out the opportunities for such moves and help to coordinate moves by those who choose to relocate among the various middle- and upper-class communities. This agency would also need to assist in the relocation process itself. Every move is difficult, but the challenges of moving out of a ghetto and into a considerably more upscale and possibly predominantly white neighborhood would be extreme. The tasks that burden every move—trips to the hardware store for light bulbs, meeting the new neighbors, enrolling the children in schools, joining a new church, knowing which social services are available—are intensified when the racial or class makeup of the new neighborhood is different from that of the old one.

Charitable organizations might be able to help with relocation, but given the magnitude of the endeavor, it will be necessary to rely on the government and its unique powers to raise and distribute funds. The relocation agency will need to be publicly funded. In addition, public funds will be necessary to enable people who were living below the poverty level to afford the rents in the receiving neighborhoods. The rent of those moving would be subsidized, though the subsidies may go directly to those providing the housing. One method of implementing this plan would be to issue housing vouchers and to require that realtors and landlords in the specially designated receiving communities accept these vouchers. Such a requirement would be only one small part of the effort needed to render it impossible for receiving communities to thwart the purpose of the relocation program, which is to create economic, and maybe racial, integration. Tough enforcement of existing antidiscrimination laws and perhaps the fashioning of new ones would also be necessary.

Any program seeking to end the dynamics responsible for entrenching the underclass will require an enormous dollar investment. The relocation program I have outlined is no exception, though the cost is in no way prohibitive. As a rough gauge, consider a 1994 effort by the Department of Housing and Urban Development (HUD) to institute an analogous but smaller, pilot relocation program. This program, called Moving to Opportunity, offered aid to families with children who were living in public housing in high-poverty census tracts within Baltimore, Boston, Chicago, Los Angeles, and New York. In each of these tracts, more than 40 percent of the residents were living below the official poverty level. Those who applied and were selected were given Section 8 rent vouchers that could be used only in census tracts with poverty rates below 10 percent. Local nonprofit organizations played a crucial role, supplying each moving family with a counselor who actively helped the family find an apartment and overcome the obstacles associated with the move. The cost of moving sixty-two hundred families was $234 million over two years.

These figures need to be adjusted to account for the scale of the program I am proposing, which would not be confined to persons living in public housing in five cities but would be nationwide in scope and available to all people living in areas marked by the high concentration of extremely poor black families. To define these areas with more precision we can require, as Moving to Opportunity did, that 40 percent of the residents in a census tract live below the poverty level. Estimating the precise number of families in such areas is more difficult. Studies based on the 1990 census indicated that more than 4.2 million blacks were living in census tracts with extremely high concentrations of poverty (more than 40 percent living beneath the official poverty line). A comparable figure based on the 2000 census is not yet available, but as an outside estimate let us assume that 6 million blacks now live in such areas. This number needs to be adjusted to account for the fact that the relocation program would be aimed at families rather than individuals. Working on the assumption that at least two persons comprise each family, and that every family chooses to move, the proposed program would embrace 3 million families. Based on the cost of the Moving to Opportunity program, we can estimate the cost of a comprehensive program at around $50 billion a year.

If anything, this figure is on the high side. It assumes that every family chooses to move, and it treats the average family as a two-member unit. Also, a number of collateral dynamics may reduce the costs once the deconcentration program is actually implemented. For example, the costs of relocation would have to be offset by savings from the hoped-for diminished need for programs aimed at community development, public housing, and perhaps even income support. Relocation will enhance access to jobs. In any event, we need to put the $50 billion figure in perspective. To do so, note should be taken of the fact that in June 2001 Congress passed and President Bush signed into law a bill reducing taxes by $1.35 trillion over the next ten years—almost three times the cost of dismantling the nation's ghettos under my proposed program.

The impact of deconcentration should not be measured only in monetary terms. Relocation runs the risk, for example, of eroding the base of various political leaders who have long served the most desperate neighborhoods. It is not entirely clear, however, that such political realignments as may occur will work to the long-term disadvantage of those now trapped within the ghetto. There is at least the possibility that their interests will be more effectively represented politically once they become members of more economically advantaged wards. Not only will the representatives of these wards have greater sway in the councils of power, but coalition building across class and racial lines may be easier. Political participation at the grass-roots level may also increase. Studies by Cathy J. Cohen and Michael C. Dawson in the 1993 *American Political Science Review* indicate that living in extremely poor neighborhoods leads to political disengagement and undermines the confidence individuals may have in their capacity to control or influence decisions of importance to the community. Although incumbents may be unseated, deconcentration may actually enhance democratic politics. Consideration must also be given to the gains in social and economic opportunities that ghetto residents who choose to relocate will enjoy. To make such gains available, and to end the oppression endured in a life confined to the ghetto, we may simply have to run the risk of altering established and all too familiar patterns of political representation.

Of even greater concern than these political realignments are the human costs entailed in the decision to move, especially the disruption of communal ties. For many living in the ghetto, the ordinary relations among neighbors have provided support and comfort over the years, and should not be treated lightly in considering the effects of relocation. Plans to transform inner-city communities into safe, flourishing environments with plenty of jobs, attractive housing, safe streets, easy access to good stores, strong schools, and all the other features of prosperous neighborhoods are often defended on the ground that they seek to end the danger and hardship of the ghetto while preserving what is good in the neighborhood. This ambition is indeed honorable, but I doubt that it can be fulfilled. Putting an end to the social dynamics that have transformed the ghetto over the last thirty or forty years into a structure of subordination would require so many deep interventions into the life of that community that it would profoundly disrupt, if not actually destroy, preexisting communal ties. The geography would remain the same, but the community would be different.

The program I envision openly acknowledges the threat to community entailed in deconcentration but allows the residents of the ghetto to weigh the benefit of the preexisting communal ties against what might be a better life for themselves and their children. Choosing to move entails a sacrifice. Many of the things that are so good about the old neighborhood, including social ties forged over decades, will be lost. But under my program the choice is vested where it belongs: in the individual family. Admittedly the choices of those most anxious to leave will affect the options of those inclined to stay, since a decision to stay will appear less appealing when many of one's neighbors have left. Such decisional interdependence, however, is inescapable, and it is not clear why the balance should be cast in favor of the status quo. All the available evidence indicates that it should not—there is so much to be gained by a move.

One follow-up study of the Moving to Opportunity program in Boston found that almost immediately after moving—within one to three years—children of the families that participated in the program exhibited "fewer behavior problems, prevalence of injuries, asthma attacks, and personal crimes." This program has not yet been in existence long enough to measure the long-term effects of moving, but another study—this time of a deconcentration program in Chicago that began in the late 1970s, in the context of a lawsuit—provides an even more useful measure of the benefits to be gained by moving from an inner-city ghetto to a middle- or upper-class neighborhood.

These studies, first published in 1991 by James Rosenbaum, involved moves from all-black, inner-city public housing projects to predominately suburban communities. Among adults who never previously held a job, those who had moved were over 50 percent more likely to become employed than those who remained behind. Among those who were children at the time of the move, 75 percent of those who moved to the suburbs were employed seven years after the move, compared to 41 percent of those who stayed; 21 percent of those who moved had jobs paying more than $6.50 per hour, compared to 5 percent of those who remained; 54 percent of those who moved went to college, compared to 21 percent of those who stayed in the city; and 27 percent of those who moved to the suburbs attended four-year colleges, compared to 4 percent of those who remained in the city.

When first reported, these findings were treated as front-page news. Yet they only confirmed what common sense told us and what every parent knows—although moves are painful, the chances for a better life and greater success can be significantly improved by moving to a better neighborhood. The ties that bind neighbors are indeed valuable, but my own sense is that most parents in the ghetto would be prepared to sacrifice them if offered a chance—a real chance—to move. Indeed, in

the deconcentration programs mentioned, the number of applicants greatly exceeded the available opportunities. In the Chicago case studied by Rosenbaum, for example, during one call-
in application period lasting only a few days, fifteen thousand
applicants called in pursuit of 250 places.

The individuals who participated in these programs were not
offered an unrestricted subsidy. They could not use the government funds to fix up their apartment or to improve security but
had to use the money to move. If given the chance, many would
conceivably prefer to stay put and spend the money for projects
they deemed important in the neighborhood, but that does not
seem likely. They would realize that too many of the dynamics—the poor quality of the schools, the movement of jobs to
the suburbs, and the prevalence of crime—are far beyond their
control. It is only fair to assume that those presently in the
ghetto would follow the path of the new black middle class,
who, once they had the means, left the ghetto. True, the burden
and the pain of moving would remain. Integration, in any form,
has never been a picnic, but neither is staying put.

JUSTICE

To put all the costs in perspective, we must come to understand
that deconcentration is required not only as good social policy
but also as a matter of justice. The costs of such programs are
indeed great, as would be the costs of any program that seeks
to tackle the problem of the underclass, but they are no greater
than those entailed in implementing *Brown* and are justified by
an analogous theory of equal protection. The dual school system of Jim Crow was condemned because it tended to perpetuate the caste structure of slavery; the inner-city ghetto today

has a similar effect, though the group subjugated is not defined, as under slavery or Jim Crow, in purely racial terms—race must be supplemented by economic and social coordinates. The subjugated group is not blacks in general but the black underclass. The inner-city ghetto stands before us as an instrument of subjugation and thus represents the most visible and perhaps most pernicious vestige of racial injustice in the United States—the successor to slavery and Jim Crow.

Presently the state does not, by statutes or regulations, confine people to the ghetto. To the contrary, through antidiscrimination laws governing employment, education, and housing, the state has helped to create the black middle class and thereby enabled some to leave. Yet for the better part of the twentieth century and before, the state played an important role in creating and maintaining the ghetto, and is thus duty-bound to use its powers to remedy the present-day consequences of that action. In the historic decision that provided the foundation of the Voting Rights Act of 1965, Justice Hugo Black emphasized that any court had "not merely the power but the duty to render a decree which will so far as possible eliminate the discriminatory effects of the past as well as bar like discrimination in the future." He was referring to the judiciary, for the duties of that institution were being contested, but the obligation he spoke of extends to all branches of government.

State complicity in the creation of the ghetto has taken various forms. Some of the state's responsibility derives from the failure, for most of our history, to prevent acts of discrimination and violence aimed at keeping blacks out of white neighborhoods. In other instances the state played a more active role, for example, by enacting racial zoning ordinances or enforcing racially restrictive covenants. Though these practices were outlawed—the first in 1917, the second in 1948—they played a crucial role in the formation of the black ghetto. Later they were replaced by the more subtle but equally pernicious practices I mentioned earlier: California's Proposition 14, restrictions on FHA loan guarantee programs, and the discriminatory methods by which public housing projects were located. The means by which residential segregation has been established and maintained in the United States—described in further detail in Douglas S. Massey's and Nancy A. Denton's important 1993 book *American Apartheid*—are as sinister, and their effects as lasting, as Jim Crow segregation in the South, especially when coupled with this country's traditional economic and social policies.

Blacks are not the only group in America that suffers from high rates of poverty and joblessness and that finds itself concentrated in neighborhoods wracked by crime and overburdened public institutions, such as the schools. Today we find in our large urban centers residential clusters of Asian immigrants or Hispanics whose economic profiles may closely resemble that of black ghetto residents. Yet an adequate assessment of the chances of these other groups for upward mobility requires a fuller understanding than is currently available of the family and kinship structures in these neighborhoods and the capacity of available intermediate institutions such as the churches. Segregation may not have the same social meaning or social consequences for these groups as it does for blacks who are poor and jobless.

Even if it does, however, the claim for justice supporting a deconcentration program aimed at the black ghetto seems more urgent simply because of the active role the state played over the last century in creating these neighborhoods. Certainly the state has an affirmative obligation to eradicate any practice or condition that systematically disadvantages a group and threatens to turn them into pariahs—even the casual passerby has an obligation to throw a drowning man a life preserver. But the state's obligation to provide a remedy is all the more powerful when it helped to bring the threatening condition into being in the first place.

The foundation, perhaps the inspiration, for a deconcentration program along the lines I envision can be traced to the 1976 Supreme Court decision in *Hills v. Gautreaux*. The case involved the Chicago Housing Authority (CHA)—the agency specifically charged with the construction and management of public housing projects in Chicago—and arose from the Authority's practice of giving local city council members the summary power to prevent the construction of such projects in their wards. It was understood that the residents of such projects would be predominantly black, and council members from white wards used their power to prevent the construction of public housing projects in their areas. As a result, for years all public housing projects in Chicago were located only in black neighborhoods and thus helped constitute the urban ghettos of that city. The Supreme Court ruled this practice unlawful and, by way of remedy, sustained an order of a lower court requiring HUD to provide funds to help break up these concentrations of poor black families.

The relocation remedy upheld in *Gautreaux* provided rent subsidies to some CHA residents, enabling them to move to suburban committees. Support was also provided to a nonprofit organization in Chicago that participated in the relocation program by looking for housing and facilitating the move. Arguably this remedy could be conceived as a form of compensation for a highly discrete act of racial discrimination, namely, the decision to locate the public housing projects only in black neighborhoods. Such a reading of *Gautreaux* would limit its scope and reduce it to a public housing precedent. But I see lurking beneath its surface a far more powerful principle: an obligation on the part of the state to eliminate a social formation that it helped create and that is responsible for producing and perpetuating the black underclass.

This principle is suggested by the fact that the remedial obligation imposed in *Gautreaux*—funding the relocation agency and providing subsidies to enable tenants to move—was placed on HUD, the federal agency, rather than on the CHA or the Chicago City Council. HUD did not participate in any way in the choice of the site for the public housing projects. At most, it could be accused of funding public housing projects with the knowledge that they were being built only in black wards. This conduct might be described as supporting or acquiescing in the discrimination, thus bringing it within the ambit of both Title VI of the Civil Rights Act of 1964 and the Constitution's equal protection guarantee. But the involvement of federal and state governments in creating urban ghettos may be similarly characterized. So may the government's role in the social processes responsible for joblessness and poverty in the ghetto, and the inferior quality of schools and social services available there.

Account must also be taken of the fact that the *Gautreaux* remedy required HUD to provide subsidies that would enable the public housing residents to move to the suburbs and to do so in a scattered fashion. These suburbs were predominantly white. A remedy conceived in purely atomistic terms—as a corrective for the race-based decision as to where to build public housing projects—could not possibly have that reach. At best, such a remedy would mandate the construction of public housing projects in white parts of the city—for example, building a counterpart to the Robert Taylor Homes in a predominantly white ward with comparable land value or a similar socioeconomic profile, and then giving all the Robert Taylor Homes residents a chance to move to this new project. The remedy approved in *Gautreaux*, by contrast, was far more ambitious: It contemplated moving the public-housing residents, all of whom were black, into middle- or upper-class neighborhoods in the suburbs and scattering them so as to avoid creating a new ghetto.

In purely individual terms, the *Gautreaux* remedy succeeded admirably. As Rosenbaum first found, the employment opportunities and educational achievements of those who had moved increased significantly. Even more remarkable, I believe, is that *Gautreaux* marked the beginning of the process of dismantling the massive public housing projects in Chicago, such as the Robert Taylor Homes, and thus represents the first decisive step toward the dissolution of the ghetto. In this respect the *Gautreaux* remedy should be seen not as a compensation for a discrete act of discrimination—an attempt to put certain persons in the position they would have been in but for a particular act of discrimination—but as a broader remedy designed to eliminate a structure of subordination that the state helped to create. *Gautreaux* was premised on an understanding of how massive public housing projects—with their concentration of poor, jobless families often unable to assist significantly in the socialization process, all sending their children to the same local school, victimized by crime and gangs—had become a mechanism that created the black underclass and threatened to perpetuate it. The *Gautreaux* remedy also constituted a recognition of the government's responsibility for dismantling that mechanism.

Although the *Gautreaux* remedy had grandiose ambitions, it was rather limited in its numbers. Only seventy-one hundred families received subsidies. This limit, I believe, was a function of the fact that the precise number of families receiving subsidies was set in a consent decree, or bargained-for agreement, between HUD and the plaintiffs. The number was not dictated by considerations of justice, which is, after all, the only proper metric for a court or any other institution bold enough to remedy a violation of equal protection. Every affirmative remedy poses the question of precise limits: How much must be spent to do justice? How much is enough? No precise response can be given to these questions at this stage other than to say that the subsidies must be large enough to relocate all residents of the ghettos who choose to move—large enough to bring an end to the social mechanism that is entrenching the black underclass across generations. Anything short of that would allow to remain in place an instrument perpetuating a hierarchical structure that is at odds with the Constitution's egalitarian aspirations.

In an attempt to minimize or trivialize deconcentration remedies, and thus to highlight his neo-WPA program and the effort to bring jobs to the ghetto, William Julius Wilson claims that the acceptability of *Gautreaux*-type integration is dependent on the modesty of its scope. "The success of this program," he writes of *Gautreaux*, "is partly a function of its relatively small size. Since only a few families are relocated to other housing sites each year, they remain relatively invisible and do not present the threat of a mass invasion." It is not at all clear what Wilson means by a "mass invasion" or whether such a threat would ever be present under a relocation strategy designed to avoid the creation of new ghettos. The approach I envision entails moving few enough ghetto residents into each middle- or upper-class neighborhood that the prior residents of those neighborhoods remain. We need to recognize, moreover, that whatever hostility this relocation program engenders—from whites in upscale communities, from blacks in such communities who pride themselves on having escaped the ghetto, or from the political or economic interests served by the perpetuation of the ghetto—it cannot be a basis for limiting the program or, even worse, turning one's back on it altogether. Justice permits no such compromise. It requires instead that the state undertake all action necessary to end "lock, stock, and barrel"—as Judge John Minor Wisdom once put it in talking of the remedies for school segregation—the social processes that continue to perpetuate the near-caste structure of American society.

PART II

DOWN BY LAW

RICHARD FORD

One must applaud Owen Fiss's admonishment to end, lock, stock, and smoking barrel, the isolation and disempowerment that currently characterizes life in America's urban ghettos. Likewise, Professor Fiss's description of the deplorable history of state-sanctioned racist policy that created and maintained the urban ghetto is a necessary but all-too-often ignored part of any policy discussion that addresses the conditions of the urban poor. This history should be part of any high school education, but distressingly few Americans know of it or care to learn. And I agree wholeheartedly with Fiss's argument that the compulsory isolation of the ghetto is morally analogous to Jim Crow segregation and that the imperative that society find and implement an effective remedy is analogous to the imperative to desegregate public schools that was (partially) addressed in *Brown v. Board of Education*.

Better yet, Professor Fiss is not content simply to describe the problem, as so many have already done. He insists that justice demands a viable solution, and his proposal—a comprehensive, although voluntary, program of relocation, funded by the state and available to anyone living in a sufficiently distressed neighborhood—is as bold and sweeping as the challenge is pervasive and daunting. Fiss faces unflinchingly the enormous cost of such a program: He recognizes that not only moving expenses for millions of families but also sizable rent subsidies of indefinite duration would be required to insure that low-income families could move to middle- and upper-income neighborhoods.

Still, it is not clear that Fiss's proposal will serve all the people he hopes to help. Fiss correctly notes that the blacks who benefited most from civil rights reform were those already well poised to do so—those with skills and education. These successful blacks left their former neighborhoods in what William Julius Wilson calls "black middle-class flight," exacerbating the isolation and powerlessness of those left behind in the ghettos. We could expect a similar result if Fiss's proposal were enacted: Those inner-city poor with some skill, experiences outside the ghetto, mainstream acculturation, and internalization of the work ethic will be more likely to take the initiative and leave the ghetto, and more likely to succeed when they do. Those worst off, both in terms of wealth and, more important, in terms of skills, will stay behind or, when they try to move, will meet with failure and alienation. They will then most likely retreat to their former neighborhoods or form new enclaves in the suburbs that will rapidly become the suburban ghettos Fiss hopes to avoid.

In this scenario Fiss's reform will, of course, have helped those who move and succeed enormously. But it will leave behind an even more concentrated, even more desperate, and even more isolated super-underclass.

All this is to say that Fiss's solution cannot be the only solution. Fiss criticizes William Julius Wilson's suggestion that public policy revitalize inner-city communities through WPA-style public investments and jobs programs. He notes that such an approach fails to reckon with the lack of work ethic that, according to both Fiss and Wilson, is pervasive in the ghetto. But Wilson's proposal does have the merit of incrementalism: He envisions providing steady work for the poor where they live and are, if not comfortable, at least familiar. Fiss, by contrast, demands that these socially isolated poor not only develop a work ethic and mainstream social skills sufficient to win them jobs in the *private* sector of a middle-class suburb but also that they do so while simultaneously acculturating themselves to a new social milieu.

Moreover, there is a serious omission in Fiss's analysis of the ghettoization dynamic. Fiss asserts that the problem of ghettoization is structural and self-perpetuating: Social and economic isolation promote joblessness, despair, and socially dysfunctional behavior, which promote poverty, which insures social and economic isolation. But he leaves out a significant element of that structure, namely, the laws governing the very middle-class and wealthy suburbs he hopes will become welcoming havens for the underclass. Wealthier suburbs have strong incentives to exclude poor urbanites and the means by which to do so, both supplied by the legal regime of American local government.

Incentives? American cities and towns in most states fund public services primarily through property taxes. They also are entitled to limit access to those services to residents of the jurisdiction. This means that cities have an overwhelming incentive to encourage in-movers who will increase the value of property (and therefore tax revenues) and consume little in services, and to discourage in-movers whose presence will decrease property values and who will need a lot of public services. It scarcely needs to be said that the urban poor fit the latter description.

Means? Although American local governments do not have explicit immigration policies, they do have broad powers to restrict land uses. By excluding all or most high-density or multi-family housing, middle-class and wealthy suburbs can effectively screen out low-income potential residents by prohibiting the housing they can afford. Local governments also can, and do, resist regional public transportation, halfway houses, group living arrangements, and rehabilitation centers—all services that many low-income people require to make the transition from troubled or dysfunctional lifestyles to success in the job market.

The engine of ghettoization is not entirely internal to the ghetto nor are its root causes exclusively historical. Although Fiss recognizes the responsibility of the explicitly discriminatory policies of the past for the present reality of the urban ghetto, he does not consider the salience of present-day public policy in reproducing the ghetto and reinforcing its borders. While Fiss's proposal is laudatory, it is incomplete. Without the reform of local policies that reinforce the isolation of the ghetto from outside, it would be like running the furnace with the windows open.

COMMUNITIES, CAPITAL, AND CONFLICTS

TRACEY L. MEARES

▣ Owen Fiss deserves the people's ovation for bringing attention to the American ghetto's persistence in the midst of a sustained period of plenty in the United States. Professor Fiss is right to bring attention to the poor, racialized spaces. He notes that "the ghetto is responsible for the creation and maintenance of the black underclass." Ghettos do more, however. Ghettos are a "race-making situation."[1] They help inform a color-coded awareness that associates African-American skin with poverty, crime, and incivility, and white skin with the opposite of these characteristics. In addition to segregating and isolating the black poor, ghettos inform stereotypes that are attached to all African Americans and, in the process, impact relationships among all Americans whatever their race.

There can be no denying that ghettos, because of what happens to those who live within them and how they influence those who live without them, are places that ought not be preserved. The question treated in the bulk of Owen Fiss's essay is how we, through government programming, ought to go

---

[1] David James, *The Racial Ghetto as a Race-making Situation: Law and Social Inquiry* 19 (1994): 413.

about the business of dismantling them. While the policy programming that underlies his proposal is complex and faces almost insurmountable political hurdles (which I will not detail
here), the proposal itself is simple. Owen Fiss advocates de-
struction of the American ghetto by dispersing those who live
there to wealthier, predominantly white communities. Professor Fiss chooses this course because he claims that the crime,
joblessness, poor housing stock, and hopeless schools found in
abundance in ghettos result from clustering groups of extremely
disadvantaged people together in one place. In pointing out
these "concentration effects," Professor Fiss joins an esteemed
group of scholars led by noted sociologist William Julius Wilson, who has advanced this thesis in at least two important
books. If concentration is the problem, then deconcentration
must be the answer, right?

Unfortunately answers to complex problems are rarely so simple. One drawback to this proposal is that it fails to recognize
adequately the potential benefits of concentration. For all the
varied troubles of disadvantaged neighborhoods, they still are
places containing valuable family and social ties. These neighborhoods also are places that hold the institutions residents care
deeply about, such as churches and other community organizations. Professor Fiss recognizes the value of these institutions,
but he abandons them much too quickly. "Some families may
turn for help to local churches, which have long been important
institutions in the black community. . . . Yet it remains doubtful
that the church can take the place of the family and supply discipline and structure to children who lack direction."

The black church is much more than a mere buffer zone. It
is an institution that helps create the kind of social capital that
makes any community work. Churches, nonprofit organiza-

tions, and other local businesses (which are admittedly too few in many disadvantaged neighborhoods) are parochial-level institutions that help facilitate the networks along which community norms are promulgated and circulated. These institutions play a critical role in maintaining the "norm highways" of neighborhood life that underlie the collective efforts neighborhood residents engage in to govern themselves through informal means—in ways that *they* prefer.

That these institutions often are not strong enough to do more of the important work they already are doing is not a reason to give up on them. Instead, government programming ought to devote *more* attention to improving the social organization of disadvantaged neighborhoods by supporting these institutions rather than supporting, for example, expensive "get tough on crime" policies. Much contemporary criminological research suggests that resources directed toward community social organization improvement rather than increased imprisonment will help to curb crime, gangs, and drugs—important issues Professor Fiss uses to justify dispersal of ghetto residents.

Another problem with Professor Fiss's dispersal proposal related to the social capital argument I have just made is his apparently unabashed preference for investments in human capital over investments in social capital. I do not believe that preservation of critical community institutions and the social capital that attends them ought to be preferred over investments in individuals. It is just not clear to me that individual investments ought to be supported at the *expense* of investments in the parochial. To do so ignores the collective nature of the political process.

Recent political achievements of African Americans certainly leave room for improvement, but the trend is, by and large, a positive one. The political gains African Americans have made are undeniably connected to the black church and to institutions related to it. Although those in higher socioeconomic groups tend to engage in political activity to a greater extent than those in lower socioeconomic groups, the sense of group consciousness developed by African-American involvement in religious institutions and civil rights institutions that were birthed by these organizations has tended to increase black political participation well above the level African-American socioeconomic status would predict.[2] It is not inevitable that these institutions would be destroyed by the policy choices Professor Fiss advocates, but they could well be unnecessarily weakened. It would be odd and ironic if the remedy to the decades of racial discrimination that created impoverished, segregated urban enclaves led to the weakening, rather than the strengthening, of black political power.

Relocators will need such power. The study by Leonard Rubinowitz and James Rosenbaum, *Crossing the Class and Color Lines* (2000), details the costs and benefits of the precise kinds of moves Professor Fiss supports. Rubinowitz and Rosenbaum found that public housing residents who moved to predominantly white suburbs had access to higher-paying jobs than they had in the city. Their children had access to better schools. All involved faced much less crime than they dealt with in the ghetto. We can hope that the broader program Professor Fiss supports is equally successful in helping relocators. But *Crossing the Class and Color Lines* also details incidents of significant racial prejudice and harassment. Mothers were humiliated in

---

[2] See Sidney Verba, Kay Lehman Schlozman, and Henry Brady, *Voice and Equality: Civic Volunteerism in American Politics* 230 (1995).

grocery stores for proffering food stamps, and their children were excluded from neighbors' homes and play dates. In one poignant episode a young girl tried to join a Brownie troop for two consecutive years but was told each time that the troop was full—a claim her mother knew to be untrue. While the authors acknowledge that these incidents are disturbing, they conclude that such events are not as dangerous to those experiencing them as the threats that families face in the city.

I want to say that this *must* be right. . . . But I must admit to my ambivalence. The kinds of exclusions the authors describe are not minor to the children involved. They stick and so must be dealt with for the decades to follow. I know a six year old who was excluded from a Brownie troop meeting that all her friends attended. She was the only African American girl in the class. She went to the meeting with all her friends after school. When she arrived, however, the troop leader (the mother of a friend) told her the troop was "full" and that she had to wait outside on the front steps until her mother arrived to take her home. I know that six year old well because she is me.

The continued reality of these kinds of exclusions requires me to pause before offering Professor Fiss a ringing endorsement. I pause not only because living through these incidents is almost unimaginably (for anyone who has never had to do so) difficult, but also because I worry that Professor Fiss's proposal may well create a political dynamic that ultimately leads us away from the institutions in the best position to help us deal with the social foundations that support these dynamics in majority white communities. The racial prejudice that suburban movers experienced are costs that must be balanced against the benefits of human capital investments. These costs have important political implications—especially if the "receiving communities" do not have the kinds of cultural and political institutions necessary to advocate on behalf of the relocators, as is likely to be true in majority white middle- and upper-middle-class communities.

Professor Fiss is likely correct that, given the choice, many poor blacks would opt to leave the troubled circumstances of the ghettos in which they live. But the real question, in my view, is whether relocators, if given an alternative, would choose the move to the neighborhoods Fiss favors, predominately white middle- and upper-class communities. I believe many would prefer another option were it available. An ideal solution to the problem of urban ghettos would offer them such a choice.

BETTER NEIGHBORHOODS?

ROBERT COLES

■ Many of us know and admire the work of Owen Fiss, and are grateful for his brilliant, wide-ranging legal scholarship that is grounded in a mind comfortable with literature and unafraid to grapple with the serious social and political matters that bear down on us Americans, for all our nation's might and wealth. As I read his essay, I was not surprised by the moral urgency that informs the question that serves as a title for what follows—here is one academic scholar who knows the oughts and noughts of constitutional law, yet dares address his readers with an aroused conscience, alert to the travails of fellow citizens who are having no easy time of it. Look at those left behind, we are urged, and try to imagine significant, if not drastic, remedial recourses for what has happened over the generations in our American cities, where (in some neighborhoods) many poor and vulnerable people live hard-pressed lives.

The gist of this essay is its answer to the question posed at its onset—a learned and privileged citizen's conviction that those who live in our urban ghettos be enabled (and thereby encouraged) to move out, lest they continue to be threatened by rampant social pathology, which is either explicitly mentioned or summoned by implication—as in references to "better neighborhoods" that are supposedly spared the errant, the fearful, the downright illegal and violent kind of life that the author hopes the African Americans who live in ghettos will have "left behind," as they journey elsewhere. This proposal—that our government convert a present status quo (the passivity of being left behind) to the activity of deliberate departure—will, in effect, be subsidized by millions of taxpayers.

I must say that I was concerned on several scores as I read this spirited exhortation on behalf of a bureaucratically assisted realignment of neighborhood populations across our contemporary urban scenes. We are asked to believe that the "better neighborhoods," the "receiving communities," are themselves without the problems that plague ghetto residents—common drug usage, willful gangs, a somewhat demoralized atmosphere. Some of us who work in the relatively well-to-do suburbs know all too well the serious difficulties to be found in those communities, though often certain aspects of psychological and moral pathology are kept under the table—the cheating and lying in big-deal schools, the widespread drug use, the bullying and intimidating by some youths of others, the drunken driving that proves fatal to those induced to go along (and, alas, threatened if they do not agree to say yes, to put themselves in those recklessly misused cars given by parents all too self-absorbed by the demands of their jobs, by the preoccupations of their "successful" lives). One asks for *context*, for a close scrutiny of what takes place in economically privileged neighborhoods, and also for a willingness to think of the serious neighborhood misfortunes, afflictions, disorders, and even calamities that afflict relatively impoverished white urban neighborhoods or those populated by Spanish-speaking people.

I could take Owen Fiss to streets in Boston where gangs prey on people down on their luck, where drugs are available almost everywhere, where a climate of futility, even despair, is to be found, where some residents wish they could get out, though some stand fast and firmly live out a sincere loyalty to a given section of the city—and where, I suspect (in South Boston, say, or Chelsea or parts of the North End or the South End) the lure of Quincy, of Everett and Marblehead, goes unnoticed, as well as the ever-present seductions of gentrification. (Talk about "better neighborhoods" that some working-class people, black and white alike, have no interest in joining!)

Speaking of the movement Fiss proposes, with his unfortunate talk of "tearing down" and "breaking up" certain ghetto neighborhoods, I have tape recorded another kind of plea for migratory possibility, albeit a distinctly qualified one, that ultimately leaves the matter of departure moot—spoken by an African American father as he contemplated the arrival of well-to-do white people not far from Roxbury streets that draw close to the South End:

> They're all dressed up and they are always trying to be fancy, and it's antique this, and antique that, and I worry that they are not interested in families—they are interested in *themselves*, in showing themselves off. That is not what I want my kids to see—I wish I could get us out of here, but hell, we were born here, my wife and I, and now our [four] children and us will stay and do our own showing off: We'll teach our kids what we believe is right and good, and we'll encourage them to act like good, God-fearing folks. It's nice to cut and run, but it's nice to dig in hard and long—to keep remembering that you stood up for who you are, and for what you think really matters in this life that the good Lord has leant you to keep.

BEYOND MORALIZING

J. PHILLIP THOMPSON

▨ Owen Fiss argues that the contemporary black ghetto is a product of "jobs [leaving] the community at the same time as the most successful left." With a high concentration of jobless individuals concentrated in inner-city communities, a "culture in the ghetto" is produced that "makes it most unlikely that a job creation program such as the one [William Julius] Wilson proposes will work." In his analysis of why firms left the ghetto, Fiss says that, given the manifest economic considerations involved, it is hard to believe that race was the only or even primary factor. Fiss's strategy is to break apart black ghettos once and for all and to disperse ghetto residents into resource-rich middle- and upper-class white neighborhoods.

I disagree with Fiss's description of how the ghetto emerged and his proposal about how it might be eradicated. I think the best place to begin this critique is with Fiss's characterization of what created the ghetto of the "underclass." Fiss argues that economics, not race, was the primary factor in making the ghetto. He points to Wilson's observations that jobs did, in fact, leave cities and that the black middle class left certain black neighborhoods as well. Fiss does not discuss at all the history of political debate surrounding these issues over the last thirty years.

His account makes it seem as though the ghetto is just a big accident that well-intentioned Americans created unknowingly. I find this hard to swallow. The civil rights movement made full employment a key issue after its legal victories over Jim Crow in 1964 and 1965. After waves of black congressmen were elected on the heels of the Voting Rights Act, they, too, focused on jobs. They linked the necessity for full employment to the need to repair the damage done by more than three hundred years of slavery and segregation. And they warned as well that a failure to act would entrench segments of the black community into perpetual poverty and despair. They demanded, thirty years ago, that African Americans not be forced to pay the price (in the form of persistent unemployment) for federal anti-inflation monetary policies. Congress mostly ignored them. The response of the American public was to elect a series of Republican presidents (with the exception of Democrat Jimmy Carter) who decimated support for cities between 1968 and 1992. Carter, it must be noted, was conservative on urban issues as well. Clinton, despite the best economy in memory, did virtually nothing to change the urban policy course that Reagan had put in place. Perhaps, as a former governor, Clinton was aware of how the Republican Party exploited anti-urban (read: anti-minority) attitudes to win control of nearly two-thirds of the gubernatorial seats in the country. Another factor in the rise of conservatism in national politics was intense local opposition to forced school integration *in the North* as well as the South. Overall, efforts to integrate schools failed miserably. Black middle-class parents seeking quality schools for their children had few options other than leaving inner-city black neighborhoods.

It is important to remember these points, because neither the exodus of jobs from cities nor the departure of the black middle class from the ghetto happened in a political and social vacuum. By separating race and economics, as Fiss does in saying that manifest "economic logic" obviates race as a cause of the ghetto, Fiss implicitly makes two assumptions. He assumes that political decisions made by government officials had no impact on economic decisions by firms on where to locate and who to hire. Second, he assumes that race did not affect these fundamental political decisions. Both assumptions are invalid. The U.S. "free" market economy is no less a state product than the former Soviet economy. The U.S. markets are no less "structured" than were Soviet five-year plans; the difference lies in how they are structured. The federal government's decision *not* to ensure full employment in response to black demands or *not* to put limits on firms' mobility despite devastating regional impacts on the rustbelt were political decisions.

Race has everything to do with politics. Nixon's appeal to the "silent majority," Reagan's visit during the 1980 presidential campaign to Philadelphia, Mississippi (site of the murder of three civil rights workers in the 1960s), Bush Sr.'s use of Willie Horton, Bush Jr.'s and McCain's deference to states' rights on the issue of South Carolina's adoption of the Confederate flag—all these are important symbolic reminders of how consistently Republicans have played the race card. Much more debilitating to African Americans, and more bipartisan, have been the attacks on "big government" and the War on Drugs.

Exactly what is "big government"? It does not mean the military or social security or tax deductions for suburban homeowners. It means programs designed to help the undeserving poor (read: minorities). Tax cuts and spending limits brought about through the revolution against big government have severely undermined the capacity of city governments to do much about poverty. Big government does not include prisons, which are a booming public/private industry. African American and Latino youth are being incarcerated en masse. Even though illegal drug usage is roughly evenly distributed across race and ethnic groups in the United States, close to 90 percent of those jailed for drug offenses are black and Latino. In some cities, more than one-third of all young black men are in jail, awaiting trial, or on probation. The vast majority are incarcerated for nonviolent drug and property offenses. Those convicted of drug crimes frequently serve long sentences. Under the mandatory sentencing guidelines of the Rockefeller drug laws in New York State, for example, an offender convicted of possessing two ounces of marijuana is required to serve fifteen years to life. The California legislature passed more than one thousand new criminal justice statutes in the late 1980s and early 1990s alone. These statistics represent a massive deployment of aggressive policing and punishment directed at black youth. Virtually no black person is immune to it, because police tactics initially employed in the ghettos, what is called racial profiling, are now employed on the nation's highways and downtown areas.

Even more alarming than the climate of terror produced by overzealous policing and the criminalization of huge numbers of nonviolent and poor black youth has been the public's acceptance of it. Since the victory of civil rights advocates in winning formal legal protection of African American citizens in the 1960s, a more effective and defensible form of racial subordination has set in, namely, racial subordination brought about through the normal mechanisms of democracy and government bureaucracy. It is not necessary for white Americans to be intense about their opposition to programs aimed at helping African Americans (or Latinos). Whites do not need demonstrations or protest movements. Since they are a strong voting majority in the nation and in nearly every state, they only need to vote. Voting is low-intensity politics. So long as white Americans are willing to tolerate a few middle-class blacks in their midst, they can absolve themselves of charges of racism. They can justify spending more on prisons than education (already a fact in some states) as giving minority youth what they deserve based on their bad behavior. Some argue that this is American egalitarianism at work. This is a lie. If bureaucratic enforcement were egalitarian, 70 percent of those jailed for drug possession would be white, and the sheer numbers involved would ruin the economy and turn the nation into a complete police state. I seriously doubt that lawmakers intend to do this or that white Americans want aggressive policing targeted against *their* neighborhoods. Arrest statistics indicate clearly that white drug users are being exempted from targeting. There seems to be an unspoken assumption that the War on Drugs is not supposed to attack the white middle class. The white public expects this double-standard *in practice*, in the selective enforcement of drug laws. This expectation of favorable treatment by government, where equal treatment with blacks and Latinos would be unthinkable, constitutes corruption of the body politic—and it is a powerful form of racism built into the normal workings of majoritarian democracy and government bureaucracy. What is most dangerous about it is precisely its normality—it does not require an abandonment of egalitarian rhetoric, nor does it require much political mobilization. Blacks are being terrorized and incarcerated en masse in a climate of public indifference.

To return to Fiss's article. I want to suggest that two cultural problems are involved in the ghetto, not just one. There is the problem of ghetto subcultures organized around gangs and prison life that is threatening to most people who live in the ghetto and harmful to the participants themselves. The second problem is the corruption of broad sections of the white public that stems from their social privileges and basic control of public institutions. It is the latter that has created and maintained the ghetto. And it is the latter that blames the fruits of its creation solely on its victims. Fiss wants to disrupt the comfort and disinterest of white suburbia. I applaud this intent. But his proposal to integrate white suburbs is far removed from political reality. White suburbia has already shown *in practice* where it stands on racial integration and poverty deconcentration. With so many of those Fiss wants to move into white suburbia coming out of prison today, it would be harder than ever to convince white communities to accept them. Trying legally to force white Americans to integrate against their will, in a country where they are a voting majority, has not worked and it will not work. In this context, strategies focused on improving conditions where people already live such as Wilson's public works jobs proposal are a lot more politically realistic than housing and school integration.

To tackle the larger issue of continuing segregation I think that more micro strategies are needed that engage whites on racial issues beyond moralizing arguments appealing to some fictional commitment to actual equality. One might want to figure out which predominantly white institutions or movements are disposed to want to fight against housing and school segregation or the mass criminalization of African Americans and Latinos and help them forge ties with groups concerned about urban poverty. Labor unions are targeting low-income minorities in organizing drives these days, and they are good institutions for engaging the race issue. It could be suggested to labor unions, for example, that building schools instead of prisons will create a lot more jobs and union members in the long and short run. Environmental groups are another potential source of support for eradicating inner-city ghettos. It might be suggested to environmentalists that the best cure for urban sprawl—air pollution and degradation of open spaces— would be to build livable dense cities, and the key to that is eradicating concentrated poverty. There is potential for real coalition building on urban issues that address groups' self-interest but also move them beyond narrow definitions of their selves to a bigger "We."

Finally, I hope that instead of telling poor blacks that they cannot afford to live with one another (as Fiss does), some kind of democratic and empowering process can be envisioned in which African Americans might be able to utilize their churches, clubs, community organizations, and other social networks to promote their own vision of how they want to live with other Americans. Fiss's proposal would all but eliminate the black urban church and would deeply damage black political efficacy. I think that this would be dangerous for African Americans. Fiss does not seem to understand this at all. He characterizes churches together with schools as "intermediate institutions" that in the suburbs "are not so heavily burdened as those of the ghetto and that are more likely to facilitate social mobility." He seems to think that churches are like public corporations where goods can be shipped around according to capacity, and output can be ranked on an economic performance sheet. That is not what black churches are. They are voluntary associations consisting of dense social networks that frequently span generations. It takes a long time to build a sense of trust, caring, and community within a church. Some churches never achieve it, and those are the failures. A church's success is not measured by how well established its members are in the economy or by how many of its youth go to college. A successful church may produce these results, but it does not follow that an unsuccessful church cannot produce these results.

Fiss suggests that entrenched poverty has corrupted the black church and that "account must also be taken of the possibility that certain less constructive characteristics of ghetto life might be replicated in the local churches—which, to some extent, reflect the culture of the neighborhood of which they are a part." Fiss gives no examples nor does he explain exactly what "less constructive" characteristics he has in mind. I can only conclude that his economic and spatial determinism has led him to indict black churches by association with ghetto poverty. I am tempted to say that, no, white churches are the corrupt failures because their entrenched wealth and privilege silenced them through centuries of brutal racial oppression. I have seen too many caring white churches, however, to warrant such a simplistic indictment by association. I will say, however, that I have not found that "ghetto" churches are lacking in moral fabric compared to their counterparts in rich neighborhoods. I bet Fiss has not either. Maybe a good place to begin a discussion of how to eradicate ghetto poverty would be to put a hold on pretensions of white middle-class moral superiority.

CREATING OPTIONS

JENNIFER HOCHSCHILD

Owen Fiss writes with elegance, moral urgency, and conceptual clarity. I agree with his premise—that wealthier Americans owe poor residents of ghettos a chance to pursue the American dream, whether because all Americans should have such a chance or because they are in the ghetto partly because the rest of us are not. I mostly agree with his strategy of offering all ghetto residents an "opportunity to leave" backed by real resources of money and appropriate attention. But I do not *fully* agree, for two reasons.

First, absent a revolution in most Americans' preferences with regard to the race and class of their neighbors, Fiss's proposal is politically hopeless. He knows that, and his essay can be read as a "what if" thought experiment. That is a worthwhile exercise, if only because it pushes readers to devise more feasible proposals. Nevertheless, a proposal with no foreseeable chance of enactment does little to benefit the people it so eloquently seeks to help, so it seems appropriate to explore slightly more realistic solutions.

The difficulty of Fiss's proposal can be illustrated by reactions to the Department of Housing and Urban Development's experiment with the Moving to Opportunity (MTO) program.

In his brief discussion of this small relocation program, Fiss does not point out the enormous political opposition it aroused in communities targeted to receive relocated families. One example: According to the *Baltimore Sun*, Sen. Barbara Mikulski, an outspoken liberal, "spearheaded a congressional effort to kill [the] program, [which] has become a lightning rod. . . . Residents and politicians in . . . Baltimore County have attacked it, saying the program will push crime into their neighborhoods." Congress eliminated the second year of funding.

HUD was politically inept in Baltimore, but the opposition lies beyond the reach of better political tactics. The idea that all ghetto residents might find a home in middle- or upper-class neighborhoods is almost certainly a nonstarter.

My second reason for demurring is substantive rather than political. Many ghetto residents might prefer to remain in improved communities rather than to move. Fiss (and I) might disagree with their reasons—distaste for integrated living, fear of the unknown, inertia. Or we might endorse reasons such as pride in a black community, historical roots, friendships, love of urban living. But ghetto residents' reasons for preferring to remain in an improved community are immaterial, because they are none of our business. Part of what it means to pursue the American dream is the right to choose where and how you want to live regardless of whether others approve of your choice. (We do not have movements urging the use of public funds to enable suburbanites to leave their sterile and morally corrupting split-level colonials.) In short, what ghetto residents really deserve is the right either to move or to stay in a community worth staying in.

That line of reasoning suggests a somewhat different use of Fiss's $50 billion per year. Let us accept his caveats about that figure and cut it in half, or in thirds. So how should we use $15–25 billion a year? I would devote up to half of Fiss's proposal to give families the opportunity to move out. *Gautreaux* and MTO show that most such families benefit enormously, as do receiving communities. But still, we cannot immediately extrapolate from those results to "the more, the better." Neither side will benefit if too many families move too quickly into the few communities that will accept them; that would simply split a few large ghettos into many small ones, which would improve matters but not as much as Fiss intends. Furthermore, *Gautreaux* and MTO show that families need substantial help in making the transition. It is likely that as we move further into the population of potential movers, we will find more and more families that experience great difficulties in moving and could even disrupt the program for others. So move some people, into as many communities as possible, with extensive services to help movers and receivers make the most of this new chance. Spend, say, $10 billion a year.

What about the other $10 or so billion a year? For both political and substantive reasons, it should be devoted to improving the lives of the majority of ghetto residents who will remain there, at least for a while. I propose to split the funds evenly between jobs and schools. A few million would take ghetto residents to the jobs that now exist in the suburbs, by dramatically improving public transportation or by providing van service regularly and frequently. The vans could also carry meals, tutors, and social service workers; there are many good uses to which a willing, but captive, audience could put an hour or two a day. A few billion should be spent on high-quality day care facilities at the job location, whether within a single large corporation or at a spot near many smaller employers. Here, too, other amenities should be available—a pediatrician, tutors for parents, social services, and so on. Perhaps some employers could sponsor charter schools on or near their premises, so parents and children could continue to be near each other all day (and, not so incidentally, out of the ghetto).

An additional few billion could be used, if necessary, for subsidies to private employers (broadly defined to include nonprofits, community service groups, even faith-based charities) to enable them to hire as many ghetto residents as possible. I would allocate as little as possible, albeit as much as necessary, to public service employment. Public service jobs have a terrible reputation among Americans, despite their purported willingness to be generous in paying for "a handup rather than a handout." And there is, in fact, a lot of room for waste, corruption, and sloth in a regime of public service jobs. So they should be reserved for the small minority of ghetto residents who are not employable in the (broadly defined, subsidized) private sector.

I would spend the remaining $5 billion a year on schooling. Despite the stunning array of proposed and implemented educational reforms, we really know only one thing about how to improve education for poor children: teach them *with* middle-class children or *like* middle-class children. Moving ghetto residents to middle-class communities, as Fiss proposes, takes care of the first route. We need to figure out just what middle-class children get in their schooling in order to follow the second route. Surely knowledgeable teachers, decent buildings, reasonably sized classes, current textbooks, functioning computers and science labs, good playing fields, and an assumption of safety and order are all necessary. Perhaps half the billions reserved for schools should buy these resources and, more important, amply reward the small number of people who know how to sustain and replenish them. In short, I would take seriously educators' desire to be treated like professionals: Give them the resources they need to practice their profession, pay them very well if they do it well, and subject them to at least some of the discipline of the market if they will not or cannot do the job reasonably well. That is largely how we, the middle class, earn our living and choose our doctors and lawyers; children in ghettos deserve at least as well.

The other educational boost that middle-class children get and poor children in ghettos often lack is the kind of close personal attention that encourages success, halts failure before it goes too far, and opens emotional, cognitive, and vocational doors. I would devote the remaining $2.5 billion or so of schooling funds to ensuring this attention to each child in a ghetto. The "I Have a Dream Foundation" (IHAD) could be a model. It provides much of what middle-class parents provide—a guarantee of a college education if the child does well in school and frequent attention from an adult who cares for the child, takes him or her to museums and beaches, runs interference when the child gets into trouble, and otherwise looks out for the child's interests. The IHAD mentor cannot substitute emotionally for a parent, of course. But the combination of personal care directed toward educational success and a school system that has both resources and incentives to promote success will do a lot for ghetto children, even those who lack good parenting. Money is necessary, though not sufficient, to attain these goals.

If Fiss relaxed the caveats on his estimate of $50 billion a year to move ghetto residents into middle-class neighborhoods, I would have no trouble budgeting more than $20 billion. The next items on my list would include physical amenities in the ghettos such as housing and playgrounds (ensuring that both have grass and flowers) and better, not just more, policing. Other readers no doubt can add to, or even substitute items on, this wish list. But my basic point should be clear: Ghetto residents deserve the same right as the rest of us to decide among decent options on where to live, and we have a responsibility to contribute the resources they need to do so. Fiss would encourage most or all to move out of the ghetto; I would encourage some to move while enabling others to sample the suburbs eight hours a day or to bring suburban amenities and opportunities into their own neighborhood. Owen Fiss and I do not, however, fundamentally disagree. If only the political debate in our nation revolved around such a relatively minor dispute over implementation!

EXIT AND REDEVELOPMENT

GARY ORFIELD

■ Owen Fiss argues that the ghettos and barrios of our metropolitan areas are profoundly harmful to their residents and to the larger community, and that radical policy alternatives would produce much better results. I agree on both points. Genuine and supported choices to move out of inner cities in a way that avoided merely extending the ghetto could produce important gains in schooling, in community opportunities, and in bringing down barriers of prejudice and opportunity. The money we are already spending on often counterproductive initiatives could be invested much more effectively, and we could be connecting many excluded families to opportunities that are critical to upward mobility in contemporary American society—better schools with better teachers, middle-class peer groups, better networks for moving into jobs and higher education, and proximity to much stronger job markets.

In fact, we are already in the midst of a gigantic relocation program of poor families from the large housing projects that are being leveled in various cities. Very strong conditions and services of the kind developed for Chicago's famous *Gautreaux* program—providing counseling, support services, and housing-search help in outlying suburban communities for residents of Chicago Housing Authority projects—should be attached to all these moves. The alternative is to create new ghettos and to overwhelm and resegregate a number of fragile integrated communities as thousands of poor minority families with housing-subsidy certificates seek housing in discriminatory markets.

A truly massive relocation program would, however, require huge investments in new affordable housing and housing-subsidy certificates, as well as massive changes in land-use controls and local rights to control housing types. And it is difficult to imagine how this could be done when both political parties are responding to suburban majorities who are hostile to such policies. Probably we would need a massive social movement, major political change, and a transformed judiciary to make such changes possible.

These steep political hurdles do not, however, prevent steps in the right direction. The first such step is to recognize that not all the positive mobility moves are outward. A significant number of our cities, for example, have areas of strong gentrification, where young urban professionals are eagerly turning previously neglected low-income areas into ultra-fashionable and expensive neighborhoods. With flexible tools and careful monitoring of housing conditions, the federal Department of Housing and Urban Development and state and local housing and development agencies, community groups, churches, and nonprofits could try to identify such areas early and obtain buildings and land for affordable and subsidized housing. With the right interventions, minority tenants could ride up with the boom. Funding for magnet and charter schools and other new school offerings could be tied to such a package to make certain that the new middle-class residents stayed in place when their children reached school age and provided the kind of opportunities that diverse schools offer to the children in the lower-priced housing. Another less costly strategy would be to intervene strongly to preserve and defend stable, middle-class integration in neighborhoods and inner-ring suburbs threatened by resegregation in their housing markets and schools. Such communities now rarely receive serious support, and the number of such communities will vastly increase in the next two decades as racial change becomes overwhelmingly a suburban story. Large-scale black suburbanization began in a few metros in the 1970s and is now occurring in many, but usually in the form of spreading segregation. The leaders of the relatively small list of successfully integrated suburbs and stable city neighborhoods that have broken the cycle of resegregation and enjoyed great economic and social success have very good ideas about what can be done at the local level and what kinds of support are needed from the schools and higher levels of government. We need a serious national debate on those issues.

Some constructive relocation initiatives are possible, then, and should be pursued. But most of us who have long been engaged in the exit versus redevelopment debates strongly believe that it is a mistake to pose these strategies as stark alternatives. The fact is that integration strategies are very unlikely to be implemented broadly enough or fast enough to solve the problems Fiss describes. But although many efforts to break the cycle of decline and upgrade in urban neighborhoods and opportunities have been ineffective, there have also been genuine successes, and important possibilities remain open. The basic foci should be on targeting communities with substantial chances for stable and economically diverse populations and making strategic investments across various functions of government and private lending to reverse moderate decline or to take advantage of neglected but real possibilities. Such an approach would, for example, give high priority to the provision of key resources such as competitive magnet schools and housing investment funds, which would keep middle-class families in the community and attract more of them. It would also increase private investment and build upward moving spirals while securing affordable housing early in the process. This approach would be very unlikely to work in long-impoverished and isolated core ghettos or barrios, but it could be very helpful in other settings. For example, communities experiencing substantial change in real estate markets but still largely owner-occupied and with a good, well-located housing stock primarily have to deal with the initial fear of transition and the practices of real estate steering to fight aggressively the appearances of urban decay that will stimulate fears about the future. If confidence can be restored and demand maintained in white as well as minority markets, the negative self-fulfilling prophecy may be replaced by beliefs that can sustain integration.

New possibilities may also arise with massive immigration and the development of multiracial communities. Much of our growth in the next half century will be nonwhite immigrants, mostly Latino and Asian. Depending on the patterns that develop, these groups may provide economically productive enclave economies and revitalize deteriorated communities. A great deal of attention should be given in the next few years to figuring out how to keep these neighborhoods open to low-income black and Latino families, and how to build stable multiracial neighborhoods and schools rather than new patterns of three- and four-way segregation. We are already well into these changes in our two largest states and the other great entry points for immigrants. So far almost no discussion or policy development has been directed toward these possibilities. These are not cases of classic black-white ghettoization, and surely new possibilities for successful diversity exist.

I agree that the historic policies have failed, that other measures are sorely needed, and that genuine choices of the kind provided to almost all whites and middle-class Asians must be made available on a substantial scale to African Americans and Latinos. We must think of our cities as having not only outward momentum of sprawl and spreading suburban rings but a variety of other trends and interfaces that offer both threats of growing problems and the possibility of better outcomes. Fiss raises a most fundamental question about the future of our overwhelmingly metropolitan society, and we must now think seriously about these issues.

RELOCATION WORKS

JAMES E. ROSENBAUM

⬛ Owen Fiss provides a compelling analysis of the problem of low-income black families. If he is right, then other reform efforts are unlikely to have much success until families can escape from poor neighborhoods. Fiss offers a compelling argument for residential mobility. Although I believe we may find other promising approaches, no other approach has such strong evidence of successful outcomes. The available evidence suggests that residential mobility is one of the most promising solutions for the multiple problems associated with urban poverty.

I have been studying Chicago's *Gautreaux* program for many years, and I have found that residential mobility can have truly impressive results in improving the lives of low-income families. In this program, low-income black families in public housing (or on the wait list) were assigned to various neighborhoods in the city or suburbs by a quasi-random procedure. Participants circumvented the ordinary barriers to living in suburbs, not by their jobs, personal finances, or values but by getting into the program and being randomly assigned to suburbs. The program gave them rent subsidies that permitted them to live in suburban apartments for the same cost as public housing. Participants moved to a wide variety of more than 115 suburbs throughout the six counties around Chicago. Suburbs with more than 30 percent blacks were excluded by the consent decree, and a few very high-rent suburbs were excluded by funding limitations. Yet these constraints eliminated only a few suburbs.

The receiving suburbs ranged from thirty to ninety minutes driving time from the participants' former homes. Although all participants came from similar low-income, black city neighborhoods (usually public housing), some moved to mostly white suburbs whereas others moved to city neighborhoods, most of which were disproportionately black. In principle, participants had choices about where they moved, but, in actual practice, participants were assigned to city or suburban locations in a quasi-random manner. Clients were offered a unit according to their position on the waiting list, regardless of their preference. Although clients could refuse an offer, few did, since they were unlikely to get another. As a result, participants' preferences for city or suburbs had no effect on their placement location, and analyses indicate that the two groups were nearly identical.[1]

This program had amazing results. Housing policy is usually narrowly viewed as providing shelter, but housing policy can radically improve people's lives. Studies of this program com-

---

[1] A study of 330 families found that the two groups were similar in age, education, marital status, long-term AFDC receipt, and second-generation AFDC receipt. See James E. Rosenbaum, "Housing Mobility Strategies for Changing the Geography of Opportunity," *Housing Policy Debate* 6 (1995): 231–70. Another study found no correlation between mothers' attributes (age and initial AFDC receipt) and placement attributes (city/suburb; the tract's percentages of those who are black, in poverty, unemployed, or of a low education).

pared family outcomes in mostly white suburbs to those in mostly black city neighborhoods.[2] One study followed children who moved in this program and found that, by the time they were young adults, those moving to the suburbs were much more likely to graduate high school, attend college, attend four-year colleges, and (if they were not in college) to be employed and have jobs with better pay and benefits. A study of *Gautreaux* mothers found that suburban movers had higher employment rates than city movers, and the difference was especially large for adults who did not have jobs before the move. A recent study, using official records of Aid to Families with Dependent Children (AFDC) receipt for all program participants, found strong neighborhood effects on AFDC receipt many years after moving.

Critics have said that most families would not remain in white suburbs. Yet recent research, which located 1,506 out of a sample of 1,507 families, found that more than two-thirds of suburb-mover families remained in suburbs seven or more years after entering them. Others have argued that such a program cannot serve large numbers of families. In order to have low impact on receiving communities, the program avoided moving more than two or three families to any neighborhood, and, in fact, it succeeded in this goal. Still, the program could be greatly expanded without having a large impact on any neighborhood. About four million people live in Chicago's suburbs, and the vast majority of suburbs are more than 80 percent white. Even

[2] James E. Rosenbaum, "Black Pioneers—Do Their Moves to Suburbs Increase Economic Opportunity?" *Housing Policy Debate* 2 (1991): 1179–1214. Leonard Rubinowitz and James E. Rosenbaum, *Crossing the Class and Color Lines* (Chicago: University of Chicago Press, 2000).

if all Chicago's public housing families were widely scattered among these suburbs, they would reduce the white proportion in any suburb by less than 2 percent.

If it is done poorly, however, residential mobility will not help families. Not all moves are beneficial. Under a federal mandate to tear down public housing, housing authorities across the country are moving thousands of families to other housing. In their haste to empty buildings, officials are not giving much thought to where families are moving. A recent study finds that families are being moved to low-income, mostly black areas, which are very similar to the neighborhoods they left. These moves are displacing families into equally bad neighborhoods that will have little benefit. In contrast, the *Gautreaux* program shows that a well-administered program can move low-income black families to neighborhoods that have positive influences, but this must be done carefully, not in a willy-nilly fashion in a short period of time.

Another limitation is that some families may not be prepared to benefit. The *Gautreaux* program had three selection criteria intended to assure landlords that they would get good tenants and make it more likely that participants would be able to remain in these apartments. The program tried to avoid overcrowding, late rent payments, and building damage by not admitting families with more than four children, large debts, or unacceptable housekeeping. None of these criteria were extremely selective. Because 95 percent of AFDC families have four or fewer children, the overcrowding restriction eliminates only a few eligible families. Moreover, *Gautreaux* administrators estimate that about 12 percent of applicants are rejected by the credit check or rental record, and only 13 percent are rejected by counselors who find property damage on a home visit. Thus all three criteria reduced the eligible pool by less than 30 percent. While these three conditions were not highly restrictive and allowed a large proportion of low-income families to be eligible, some families were excluded.[3]

In contrast, a front-page article in the *Chicago Tribune* recently described a residential mobility program that included some families with histories of property vandalism and crime who were being moved into private apartments. Even though such families may not be typical of housing project residents, landlords will be reluctant to lease to families in that program. Failure to screen out families who are unprepared for the move, or failure to give them appropriate preparation, may doom many families to failure while stigmatizing the entire effort. Social policy cannot simply gloss over these difficulties. Families with poor housekeeping skills, poor rent-paying histories, large outstanding debts, destructive family members, or active criminal involvement will make poor tenants and will be evicted. Programs that go to great expense to move such fami-

---

[3] *Gautreaux* participants are similar to a random sample of Chicago AFDC recipients in their length of time on public assistance (about seven years) and their marital status (about 45 percent never married and 10 percent currently married) S.J. Popkin, "Welfare: A View from the Bottom," unpublished Ph.D. diss., Northwestern University, 1988). But *Gautreaux* participants are less likely to be high school dropouts (39 percent pre-move versus 50 percent), tend to be older (median age of thirty-four versus thirty-one years), and have fewer children (mean of 2.5 versus 3.0). Still, they are more likely to be second-generation AFDC recipients (44 percent versus 32 percent). In sum, although *Gautreaux* participants may be of slightly higher socioeconomic status than the average public assistance recipient, most differences between them are not large.

lies and compel landlords to accept them will waste money and damage political support. Residential programs must have appropriate selection criteria.[4]

These programs can be combined with other programs to address these problems, for example, courses to teach housekeeping skills, credit management, and so on. Moreover, if low-income families are given incentives for meeting the selection criteria, they will have reason to alter their behavior. If such steps are taken, programs may not need to compel landlords to accept program participants. After a few years of operation, Cincinnati's HOME program reports that landlords telephoned to request participants whenever they had a vacancy. The program became a preferred provider of tenants. While landlords knew that program participants were low-income blacks, they knew that they were screened on appropriate criteria and that prior participants had turned out to be good tenants. Landlords could not get such assurances from strangers who answered their newspaper ads.

The *Gautreaux* experience suggests that if residential mobility programs are careful to select (or prepare) families and to place them in appropriate areas, they can have truly impressive benefits. Just as Fiss indicates, residential moves lead to remarkable changes of life circumstances, and these changes have dramatic benefits on people's behavior. Housing policy can do more than provide shelter—it can radically improve people's lives.

---

[4] James E. Rosenbaum and Shazia Miller, "Certifications and Warranties: Keys to Effective Residential Integration Programs," *Seton Hall Law Review* 27 (1997): 1426–49.

UNLIKELY TIMES

ALEXANDER POLIKOFF

To criticize Owen Fiss's essay—"What Should Be Done for Those Who Have Been Left Behind?"—will inevitably smack of ingratitude. What Fiss argues—that America must break up its black ghettos for both justice and social policy reasons, and that we possess a feasible means for doing so—can hardly be said too often. At best the argument has been, and following September 11 is likely to continue to amount to, no more than a whisper on the national political stage. More whispering should not be gainsaid.

Yet if someone of Fiss's stature—he has been described as one of the country's leading constitutional theorists—unexpectedly chooses to devote himself to this chronically mismanaged corner of American social policy, one might have hoped for more than is offered. (We might, for example, have been given a game plan for how to cross the threshold issue of political will.) To look on the bright side, however, its very brevity and inattention to detail will perhaps give the Fiss statement an accessibility and a "purity" that may generate more interest than a fuller treatment would have. Nearly a quarter of a century ago I wrote an entire book, subtitled "The Case for Heroism," making the very argument Fiss now remakes. The ensuing silence was deafening.

First, to the positives. Fiss rightly gives short shrift to those who romanticize the "community" and "culture" of the ghetto, and contend that we should fix it up rather than tear it down. Yes, Fiss acknowledges, individuals—James Baldwin is Fiss's example—can emerge like tempered steel from ghetto beginnings. But, for most, the ghetto has been and is a destroyer of lives. The typical ghetto product is not Baldwin but a drug pusher, a prison inmate, or the young Pharaoh in Alex Kotlowitz's *There Are No Children Here* (1991), who sat on his bed one day and cried because he might never get out of the "projects." Or James Howard, a young friend of Pharoah's brother, whose family did manage to get out and who for months thereafter "knelt at his bedside before he went to sleep and prayed that God would not make him move back." (There is a certain hubris in the argument of the romanticizers, many of them academics, who, because of their view of where ghetto dwellers should want to live, would deny the Pharoahs and James Howards a choice in the matter.)

Fiss also rightly rejects the argument that the ghetto is fixable, with enterprise zones, government job programs, charitable activity, criminal justice reform, and the like. The evidence, even during the boom decade of the nineties, is conclusively to the contrary.

Fiss's emphasis on justice is another plus. The black ghetto, Fiss says, is "the most visible and perhaps most pernicious vestige of racial injustice in the United States—the successor to slavery and Jim Crow." And it didn't just happen. Much less did it come about because, like first-generation immigrants, blacks wanted to cluster together—a bromide that even today is offered in some academic pharmacies. The incontestable historical fact is that, as the Kerner Report said as long ago as the sixties, white society deliberately created and has deliberately maintained the black ghetto.

Surprisingly, given that justice is his strong suit, Fiss pulls his punch. The federal government did not just "actively support" exclusionary practices. Rather, it led the New Deal–shaped housing industry in creating the pervasive dual housing market that has plagued us for the entire half century since the Second World War. And the federal government did not just make it "initially impossible" for blacks to get mortgages in white neighborhoods; it denied them in black neighborhoods, too, condemning blacks not only to segregated but also to inferior housing. The fact is that governments, including the federal government, first condoned the ghettos created by private citizens and the real estate industry and then, in a variety of ways, effectively gave them the force of law. As historian Arnold Hirsch puts it in *Making the Second Ghetto* (1983), "The implication of government . . . was so pervasive, so deep, that it virtually constituted a new form of de jure segregation."

It is when Fiss turns to the remedy—a housing mobility program offering rent subsidy tickets out of the ghetto to those who want them—that the Fiss essay is disappointing.

Fiss contends that we should designate "receiving communities" and require realtors and landlords within them to "accept these vouchers." This is no longer asserting a principle of justice but recommending a specific implementation technique. Almost certainly, in its "designation" of communities and "requirement" of voucher acceptance, it is an unwise one. A bit of history explains why.

By the time the civil rights revolution of the early sixties petered out in white backlash, black power, urban rioting, and Vietnam, truly important gains had been achieved. De jure segregation and Jim Crow were dead. In schools and other public facilities, in voting rights and jury service, revolutionary change had been wrought.

Not so in housing. Even in 1964 the high point of federal commitment to civil rights, when the nation's first southern president in a century was intoning, "We shall overcome," the National Committee Against Discrimination in Housing said: "Today, in the very eye of the storm of the Negro revolution, the ghetto stands—largely unassailed—as the rock upon which rests segregated living patterns which pervade and vitiate almost every phase of Negro and Negro-white relationships."

Four years later, after rioting by blacks in more than two dozen cities had rocked and frightened the nation, the Kerner Report warned that underlying forces leading to civil disorder were continuing to gain momentum. The "most basic" force, it said, was "the accelerating segregation of low-income, disadvantaged Negroes within the ghettos of the largest American cities."

Then, for a brief, unbelievable moment—under, of all people, recently inaugurated Richard Nixon—the nation seemed poised to do something about its ghettos. In January 1970 George Romney, Nixon's first secretary of Housing and Urban Development (HUD), pronounced that it was vital for subsidized housing to be dispersed more broadly than in the past. That April Nixon appeared to support Romney's emerging policy. "There must be an end," said the President's Report on National Housing Goals, "to the concentration of the poor in land-short central cities, and the inaccessibility to the growth of employment opportunities in suburban areas." The objective was to achieve "open communities" that provided jobs and housing for families of all income levels and races. To that end, legislation would be introduced to prohibit local governments from discriminating against federally subsidized housing. Whereupon, as "a necessary first step in ending the ominous trend toward stratification of our society by race and by income," Romney sent to Congress a proposal to empower the federal government to override local ordinances that excluded federally subsidized housing.

But the unbelievable moment was just that. When the inevitable local opposition appeared, Nixon ducked, Romney was defrocked, and the proffered legislation was deep-sixed. In a televised press conference, followed by a formal Presidential Statement on Equal Opportunity in Housing, Nixon told the country, "I believe that forced integration of the suburbs is not in the national interest." By choosing the "forced integration" phrase, said the *Wall Street Journal*, the president knocked the props out from under George Romney and "draped the dreaded race-mixing shroud over the entire Romney effort to move subsidized housing beyond city limits."

Thus ended the first and last serious effort of the executive branch to deal with what Romney (and the Kerner Report and Gunnar Myrdal before him) had called the nation's most serious domestic issue. Congress, increasingly dominated by white suburbia, was not—absent presidential leadership—a candidate for dispersing the ghetto. And in 1974 the door to the judicial branch was slammed shut when the Supreme Court, in a 5–4 decision, ruled that suburban school districts could not be required to help desegregate Detroit's nearly all-black schools.

The point of this historical recollection is twofold. First, possibilities for moving toward justice may come at unlikely times. (A Nixon administration. A Bush administration?) Second, they are characterized by extreme fragility. (The Romney initiative was snuffed out in an instant.) These are lessons to bear in mind as we read Fiss's essay. For so far as ghetto busting is concerned we do not quite remain stuck where we were in 1974. In the year of the disastrous Detroit school decision, Congress (thanks ironically to Nixon) enacted the very rent subsidy program Fiss embraces as his mechanism for doing justice. In the ensuing quarter century, the mechanism has been explored and tinkered with and has gained some credibility. Studies show good results from "mobility." HUD is now well along in a ten-year, five-city demonstration program called Moving to Opportunity (MTO), whose preliminary results are likewise encouraging. A major half-way point evaluation is already under way. One can imagine (fantasize?) that, if the evaluation is positive, the time will be ripe for mounting the argument in support of exactly the housing mobility remedy Fiss espouses.

A second development, in addition to Moving to Opportunity, also supports the hope that a new day may be coming. In the early and mid-nineties Congress told public housing authorities to dismantle the worst of their public housing ghettos. Though the laws do not apply to all ghettos (that is, urban communities with more than a 40 percent poverty population, whether or not they include public housing), these enclaves of poverty and segregation are good places to start. Because the development of mixed-income communities on the sites of demolished public housing buildings will include fewer public housing units than those torn down, many of the relocated families must move via rent subsidies into private housing—an impetus to enlarge Fiss's proposed remedial program.

What Fiss does not say—surely his wisdom and eloquence would be most helpful here—is how to help us seize the opportunity that, just possibly, is coming. If the MTO evaluation is positive, we may find ourselves in one of those rare moments when ghetto policy planets are lined up in a favorable configuration. At such a time, if any new social policy initiative can make its way through antiterrorism funding, we will need not only the eloquence of our Owen Fisses but their practical wisdom as well to steer the bark of just social policy through the numberless coral reefs—"big government" and "social engineering" critics, Not in My Backyard (NIMBY) activists, and black anti-integrationists, to name but a few—lurking to wreck it.

AGAINST SOCIAL ENGINEERING

JIM SLEEPER

If the state in our vaguely liberal-capitalist regime really did maintain "ghettos" as "structures of subordination" or subjugation, as Owen Fiss insists, then the remedy might indeed be a massive public program to move millions of people into other millions of people's neighborhoods in the expectation that hearts and minds would follow. But we do not live in such a society. The word *"ghettos"* has fallen from use partly because desperate, inner-city tracts are less creations of state policy than artifacts of a confluence of actions too complex for policy makers to design, let alone understand. Since the First World War, black sharecroppers and their children have flooded to the North seeking work and finding more white racism; since the Second World War, real estate developers, auto manufacturers, and the state joined to create the vast market and myth of suburbia, which deepened "underclass" isolation. So did massive shifts in industry, and hence jobs. As all this was happening, urban real estate speculators paid off government to ignore (or sometimes, under ambitious but misguided liberal Democrats, to subsidize) a lot of profiteering on white racism and black poverty.

To call what resulted a state-run "structure of subordination" is to indulge a moral flight of fancy about these myriad decisions and events. Since the causal role of public policy in it all is not so simple, neither is the public role in a remedy. If I may transpose the words Fiss used to dismiss sound strategies for inner-city redevelopment, his ambition of helping poor, black, inner-city residents through a $50-billion-a-year relocation to more stable communities "is indeed honorable, but I doubt that it can be fulfilled." I say that for two reasons.

First, any social engineering that discounts, as Fiss does, the postwar experiences and aspirations of the families now living in his intended "receiving communities"—that is, of more than half of all the households whose cooperation his program would require—will only revive the dynamics of real estate, race, and politics that defined those "receiving communities" to begin with. We had better first study urban postwar history not from the bottom up but from the near-bottom up—from the hidden injuries and imperatives of homeowners in "receiving communities" whose own parents fled the very inner-city tenements whose current poor residents Fiss now orders them—and I do mean "orders" them—to receive. Anyone who has lived and studied that history will find it hard to comprehend an idea of Justice (unless it be criminal justice) that ignores more than half those who must be parties to its implementation.

Second, such a relocation program would undercut far more nuanced inner-city redevelopment schemes, social and economic, whose possibilities have been demonstrated and which, in places like the South Bronx, have already had dramatic effects. Fiss's proposal reads as if these efforts and the more complex challenges and opportunities to which they respond were utterly unknown. To understand them, we need to unlearn much of what we thought we knew about government's capacities in a civic culture that rests on constitutionally impregnable associations of private property with radical individualism and speculative investment. We ought to suspend our search for legal precedents for massive public programs and ponder instead what such past programs teach us about the laws of unintended consequences and costs of good intentions. We cannot hope to advance a politics or a policy that assigns to the state both the burden of guilt and the burden of redemption.

Let me sketch what we too often ignore by saying something, first, about the "receiving community" residents, who are invisible in Fiss's proposal and, second, about deft initiatives and new learning curves involving urban actors who are cooperating, at last, to win constructive leverage in seemingly frozen inner cities.

A FORGOTTEN EXODUS

Fiss's proposal would "require that realtors and landlords in the specially designated receiving communities" accept rent vouchers as "only one small part" of a determined effort "to render it impossible for receiving communities to thwart the purpose of the relocation program . . . to create economic, and maybe racial, integration." Naturally, "tough enforcement of existing antidiscrimination laws and perhaps the fashioning of new ones would also be necessary." And Fiss would defy "whatever hostility this relocation program engenders—from whites in upscale communities [or] from blacks in such communities who pride themselves on having escaped the ghetto"—on the grounds that "justice permits no such compromise. It requires instead that the state undertake all action necessary to end 'lock, stock, and barrel'—as Judge John Minor Wisdom once put it in talking of the remedies for school segregation—the social processes that continue to perpetuate the near-caste structure of American society."

I will pass over Fiss's resort to the aptly named John Minor Wisdom's firearms metaphor and over the fate of school-segregation remedies that actually accelerated school segregation, swelling Michigan's Macomb County and much of New Hampshire with defectors from busing's "receiving communities" in Detroit and Boston. Let me acknowledge, instead, that something like a massive national (though not just "government") program did create the receiving communities themselves. The children of white-ethnic and Jewish immigrants rode the G.I. Bill, Federal Home Administration mortgage subsidies, and new interstate highways en masse to suburbia. These initiatives came partly at the behest of the real estate and auto industries, and were justified by legislators in the name of national defense. (Americans seem unable to undertake great social initiatives except in the shadow of "war" and metaphors about firearms. Some of the early rhetoric that justified urban renewal and, later, the War on Poverty illustrates this tendency.)

Who are the residents of Fiss's intended "receiving communities"? Aside from his passing reference to people "who pride themselves on having escaped the ghetto," I find no notice of how they have weathered the Lockean currents of real estate speculation and mobility (geographic and economic, upward and downward) that shape this country's political and civic life. Yet the effects of these odysseys are seared into the histories and reckonings of working- and lower-middle-class people, black now as well as white, whose families lived (and were disdained and exploited) in the very tenements now occupied by

the objects of Fiss's moral concern. Nothing is said about integration as a two-way process that comprehends the "receiving"
families' own flights from inner cities.

Some of these were really more like migrations, prompted in
the fifties by the artfully marketed and subsidized attractions
of suburban green pastures. Others were driven by justified
fears of the violence and property devaluation that accompanied
racial "neighborhood change" itself, driven by the speculators
cashing in on the mutually reinforcing dynamics of white racism and black poverty. It is a process I portray intimately in
chapters 4 and 5 of *The Closest of Strangers* (1990). Whites in
racially changing neighborhoods encountered rises in crime
and other social disintegration and in speculative activity by
real estate operators that threatened their property, "destroying"
market values deliberately by scaring homeowners to sell for a
song ("blockbusting"). These whites were pawns, too, driven
not by the state—at least not until big-government liberals got
into the act with busing, urban renewal, and mortgage insurance—but also by market and cultural forces they could not
have hoped to untangle.

Fiss would offer no funding, insurance protection, or counseling to the mortgage-poor refugees of these processes whose
life savings and retirement plans are still bound up in the property values of their little row houses, bungalows and suburban
six-room ranch Ponderosas with split-rail fences out front. In
the name of Justice, he would "designate" them, "require" them,
"render it impossible" for them "to thwart," and ensure "tough
enforcement" of "economic, and maybe racial, integration."
While he is at it, why not amend the Constitution to enjoin
the residents of designated "receiving communities" from moving out, as their parents and grandparents did from the inner

cities? Would passing such a constitutional amendment really be any more absurd than ordering hard-pressed homewners in Arlington, Massachusetts, or Arlington, Virginia, to welcome neighbors who are being subsidized to live next door?

"We can ignore these facts [about the social capital invested in white-ethnic neighborhood insularity] and continue to blow the trumpet for moral reaffirmations," warned the redoubtable community organizer Saul Alinsky thirty-five years ago, "but unless we can develop a program which recognizes the legitimate self-interest of white communities, we have no right to condemn them morally because they refuse to commit hara kiri." Mario Cuomo, who entered politics by mediating a conflict over New York City's effort to site low-income blacks in a white, home-owning neighborhood in the early seventies, wrote *Forest Hills Diary* to explain why massive efforts to integrate by fiat and big subsidy are doomed.

Although the Forest Hills dispute involved high-rise concentrations that Fiss foreswears, Cuomo is worth heeding: "The very idea of scatter-site was . . . virtually untested . . . and the attempt to move on it massively in several different locations appears . . . to have been a great error, no matter how noble the intentions." Why so? "Most people thought it was blacks against whites," Cuomo told me in 1989, "but a lot more of it was poor, welfare against middle class. When [low-income housing was proposed for] Baisley Park, where the black middle class was controlling the entire community, they were more ferocious about resisting the black poor than Forest Hills was. . . . So what does that say?"

What it suggests, at least, is that Fiss overestimates the replicability of successful relocation programs like that arising from Chicago's *Gautreaux* case, which succeeded only because ferocious "receiving community" opposition kept it so small and guarded that it selected the most capable, motivated applicants. Fiss wants to thwart such opposition. But if he can deride inner-city "neo-WPA (Works Progress Administration)" jobs programs as "tinged with the stigma our society associates with any government handout," what can he say of his proposed handouts to relocatees?

ANOTHER WAY

When the Industrial Areas Foundation's Nehemiah program built thousands of private, low-priced row homes in depressed New York neighborhoods, one-third of the postal and transit workers and nurses' and teachers' aides who bought them came from nearby public housing projects where they had accumulated nest eggs which they decided to invest in their "ghetto" districts. Many poor, inner-city residents do want to move out completely; perhaps, a decade from now, they will even include some of the first Nehemiah homeowners, and they should be assisted and defended in their efforts to move. But perhaps we will find that the great postwar lunge toward suburban myths and markets actually deflected or suppressed widespread yearnings for an urbanity more nuanced than developers and planners understood. Scratch many a white suburbanite, too, and you will find someone who would have preferred the decent, prosaic density of an urban neigbhorhood but felt pushed out by deteriorating housing, services, and crime. "This wasn't some neutral process whereby people decided to leave," says Paul Grogan, former president of the Local Initiatives Support Corporation (LISC), which has raised billions of dollars for urban redevelopment by helping big corporations take advantage of targeted tax credits and backing up community developers. His point is that powerful actors and interests decided in the postwar years that people should leave.

Now those actors are learning to undo old equations that drove their decisions. Thousands of urban community corporations, working with foundations, banks, and local officials, are puncturing old myths about why their neighborhoods became pits of underclass desperation. They lure bankers, their regulators, federal and state tax collectors, and developers into new coalitions of mutual interest that build or rebuild hundreds of thousand of units of affordable housing and attract the supermarkets and retail outlets that give kids footholds on the job ladder. I once accompanied Grogan and Bill Clinton's treasury secretary, Robert Rubin, on a tour of such efforts in the Bronx. Rubin is now chairman of LISC, headquartered in New York, whose efforts around the country we ought to study and support.

Fiss does rightly acknowledge something about inner-city development which busing, welfare rights and "community control" activists did not: Emphasizing race and racism has not been a good proxy for class struggle, no matter how much capitalism has exploited differences in color. Too many whites have struggled too hard for what they achieve to be willing to share it with anyone who is not working even harder. And American capitalism has proved protean, supple, and absorptive enough—often maddeningly so—to shuffle the racial deck and exploit people more randomly across old, familiar barriers of color and caste. Whether this is a real improvement is a subject for another time. The point is that very large numbers of blacks (and other nonwhites) are getting just as much as whites by working just as hard. (In New York City's Queens, two-income black households earn more than white counterparts.) Blacks are even reaping the grudging, long-overdue respect that accrues to those who keep steady on the first rungs of a job ladder.

Real estate markets in a Lockean liberal democracy will remain inextricable from bigotry, snobbery, and subtler needs to "keep up with the Joneses." But increasingly those markets will be creatures of class more than race. The more fluid and racially ecumenical the economy becomes, the more important it is to bridge the distances between poor, inner-city blacks and workplaces—but less important to rely on a massive, public relocation program to do so. It would be far better to improve public transit and the educational and social preparation without which few moves to the suburbs are sustainable. That the prospects of inner-city dwellers do rest on jobs may make my emphasis on prior urban educational and social preparation seem a Catch-22. But I think we underestimate the readying potential of new and old inner-city education models, from Catholic to charter schools, and of housing and economic developments that have finally struck a smart balance between private and public investment.

It may be a tragedy of our political culture that, even leaving race aside, big-government programs can override caste differences en masse only in the shadow of war; or it may be a renegade strength of this society that it relies so much on the fluidity of markets and the unpredictability of individual initiative. Whatever the case, we should encourage and protect inner-city residents who want to move, provided they are more or less ready. But we should recognize that the readying process—which poor immigrant urban neighborhoods did and still do provide—depends, in African-American and some Hispanic neighborhoods, on a smarter mix of for-profit, nonprofit, and local government resources in the places where they now reside. Only in this way can we hope politically, legally, and even morally to guarantee that lower-caste Americans who do get the requisite credentials and socialization are not thwarted. We might even be surprised to find that if the new strategies of inner-city redevelopment work, fewer people of all colors would want suburban Ponderosas. They and we might discover that there are better, more urbane ways to live.

IF BALDWIN COULD SPEAK

STEVEN GREGORY

One might structure a response to Owen Fiss's proposal for a large-scale deconcentration of the nation's ghettos in a number of ways. One approach would be to take it on its own terms, that is, to accept its foundational assumptions about the problem of inner-city poverty and to evaluate the proposed solution. One might then move on to consider the economic and political feasibility of relocating some six million African Americans from inner-city communities to middle-class suburbs at a cost of $50 billion per year. However, I had trouble getting my mind around this scheme. Six million people is a lot of people, and $50 billion is a lot of money in a nation that has fought tooth and nail against racial integration and resisted the use of public resources to redress social inequalities, let alone those facing people of color. In the wake of conservative and neo-liberal attacks on the welfare state, Fiss's proposal strikes me as utopian and curiously naïve. For though I am not a defeatist, I had a great deal of difficulty imagining whence political support for such an effort would come. And it strikes me as both odd and significant that Fiss does not direct attention to this critical question.

For this reason, among others, I cannot take Fiss's proposal as a realistic and carefully considered strategy for addressing the persisting poverty and inequality facing people in inner-city communities. And I will not work through the hand wringing issues of feasibility, both practical and political, that this proposal certainly invites. Rather, I would like to direct attention to how Fiss defines the nature of the problem facing the black poor in American society. I want to suggest that it is the manner in which the problem of black poverty is ideologically framed, rather than a lack of viable solutions, that is the real stumbling block to solving the problems of the inner cities. Let me try to summarize the author's point of view on the problem itself.

Fiss points out that the nation's urban ghettos are the result of systematic policies of racial discrimination in employment, housing, education, and so on—facts that are well documented and beyond dispute. Citing William J. Wilson's groundbreaking research, Fiss argues that the concentration of poor, black families in ghetto areas exacerbated the conditions of black poverty, as did changes in the structure of the U.S. economy and the spatial location of job markets. Consequently ghetto communities—particularly those in which 40 percent of people live below the poverty line—suffer from a variety of all-too-familiar problems, problems that Fiss and others contend are perpetuated by the concentration and isolation of the ghetto poor, or underclass. For these reasons Fiss concludes,

> Any ameliorative strategy must confront the fact that the ghetto is more than a place where the underclass happens to live. It is a social structure that concentrates and isolates the most disadvantaged and creates its own distinctive culture, and thus is integral to the perpetuation of the underclass.

We must pay attention to language here. As an anthropologist I take the concepts *social structure* and *culture* quite seriously: They are complex analytic categories that we use to interpret and represent fundamental differences and similarities between human groups and social systems. Moreover, assertions of cultural and socio-structural difference, often based on less than rigorous social research, have been used throughout history to explain, legitimate, as well as de-politicize social inequalities. It was the culture of the Irish, for example, that made them unfit for urban life in the eyes of some nineteenth-century thinkers. So we would do well to consider exactly what Fiss means when he refers to the social structure of the ghetto and its distinctive culture.

From what I gather, Fiss's analysis of ghetto social structure is based on what are by now familiar characterizations of black, inner-city life that center on the prevalence of single-parent or, more to the point, female-headed households. The argument is that such households, especially those headed by the notorious "teenage mother," do not possess sufficient resources to prepare children for the world of work and to provide role models that would instill in them positive social values, aspirations, feelings of self-worth, and so on. To make matters worse, the institutional resources of the ghetto (what Fiss calls "intermediate institutions"), weakened by the exodus of black, middle-class families, are ill equipped to provide surrogate parenting and socializing services. For example, noting the achievements of some black ministers, Fiss writes of ghetto churches today: "Even those churches that are located in the ghetto and draw their membership from the neighborhood cannot fully compensate for the limits of the local family as a socializing institution nor combat the destructive dynamics of the ghetto."

The social scientist in me would like to know to *which* churches Fiss refers and in *which* communities they are located.

Does it not matter? Are we to understand that such neighbor-hoods as Harlem in New York City, Compton in Los Angeles, and Liberty City in Miami have more or less the same social structure, despite significant differences in development his-tory, ethnic composition, job markets, and links to the wider urban economy and polity? One might take issue here with Fiss's assessment of the contemporary role of the black church and, more generally, of the social resources of *specific* inner-city communities. There certainly is enough evidence in the scholarly literature to challenge such generalizations. But I be-lieve it is more important to call attention to the narrative ease with which Fiss makes this assessment: how, for example, the author feels fit to dismiss the civil rights movement [read: black political activism] so easily and metaphorically as having "lost much of its steam."

One problem here is that the fuzzy notion of the "ghetto" and its conceptual cronies—teenage mother, social isolation, underclass—have achieved such symbolic currency in Ameri-can society that they can be used to typify conditions in black communities, irrespective of their historical and socioeconomic differences, let alone existing social realities. The chain of rea-soning is by now rote: Female-headed households produce failed families, which weaken social institutions, which isolate and disorganize communities, and this equals "ghetto social structure." Our understanding of the urban poor, it would seem, does not require the methodological rigor or conceptual clarity of the social sciences. Indeed, it troubles me that Fiss makes little effort to ground his model of the ghetto social structure in the scholarly literature, which has deepened our understand-ing of not only black poverty but also the structure and re-sourcefulness of black domestic groups, female-headed or otherwise. Instead, Fiss invites us to accept what have become commonsense (in the Gramscian sense) caricatures of black social disorganization and family pathology that rest on class and gender-skewed definitions of what a functional family is. In this view, as many have demonstrated, the male-headed and typically middle-class, nuclear family is taken to be the normative ideal against which the viability and pathology of other household forms is measured.

Fiss's model of ghetto social structure supports a timeworn argument about ghetto cultural distinctiveness, popularized decades ago by the notion "culture of poverty." In this theory, chronic and widespread unemployment, coupled with the breakdown of the family and social institutions, leads to a weakening of positive social values, particularly those associated with work and self-discipline. Since children in ghetto areas are socialized around people who are chronically unemployed, the argument goes, negative attitudes, habits, and behaviors regarding work are transmitted socially and across generations, producing a "cycle" of poverty. Fiss rekindles this view in order to argue the futility of efforts aimed at developing inner-city communities.

For example, challenging Wilson's appeal for a WPA-like job creation program, Fiss argues:

> Job creation in the ghetto must not only overcome the reluctance of any particular individual to accept a menial job but must also reckon this individual's membership in a community or group of similarly situated individuals. Together, *these individuals exert pressure on one another and produce a culture in the ghetto* that makes it most unlikely that a job creation program such as the one Wilson proposes will work. (My emphasis.)

Let me be candid here: How does Fiss know this? This "most unlikely" conclusion appears to rest, at best, on nothing more than speculation and, at worst, on age-old stereotypes regarding the work attitudes of the "undeserving poor." If, indeed, an anti-work culture exists in the nation's inner cities, one in which residents dissuade one another from seeking menial jobs (flipping burgers, notwithstanding), then it would need to be demonstrated with a bit more sociological rigor.

But there is more at stake here. Fiss also uses this notion of ghetto culture to support the peculiar claim that the ghetto *itself* has become a "structure of subordination." Elsewhere Fiss writes that the ghetto "is the *paramount* mechanism through which a *historically* subordinated group continues to be kept far beneath others in terms of wealth, power, and living standards" (my emphasis). Here again language is important. Are we to believe that the complex structures of racial discrimination—in housing, employment, banking and mortgage lending, policing, delivering schooling and other public services, and so forth—that have led to the formation of urban ghettos have changed? And are we to believe that it is now the culture and social structure of the ghetto *itself* that is the problem—the successor to slavery and Jim Crow? If I read Fiss correctly, this is what he is suggesting. For why else would black people be invited to abandon their continuing struggles for social justice in their communities, to sacrifice political resources that have taken decades, even centuries, to achieve, and relocate elsewhere? In a nutshell, Fiss's diagnosis of the problem of the ghetto depoliticizes poverty and elides contemporary social inequalities by—to muster another timeworn phrase—blaming the victim. African Americans might have been historically subordinated, Fiss concedes, but today it is their own communities that are the paramount structures of their oppression.

This brings me to what is perhaps the central point of my essay. By proposing mass relocation as the only viable solution to inner-city poverty, Fiss ignores the ways that the black poor *themselves* have defined the problems facing their communities and struggled to address them. To be sure, if one accepts Fiss's faceless portrait of ghetto social structure and culture, then the question of what six million black people want for themselves is moot—overshadowed by the specter of "the ghetto" and its disorganized "underclass." For from this vantage point, the black poor do not have the social or cultural wherewithal to comprehend their predicament, let alone work toward improving it. Such a conclusion, however, flies in the face of African-American history as well as the ongoing struggles for social justice that are taking place in black communities across the nation—in communities that have names, such as Brownsville, Compton, and Liberty City. I will note only one of these struggles: the Coalition to Protect Public Housing's campaign to save affordable public housing in Chicago.

In a 2000 newsletter the Coalition arrived at a position on relocation very different from Fiss's. It is worth quoting at length.

> The residents of public housing find themselves caught up in the whirlwind of changes. The fact that they are predominantly African-American has meant that the old system of racial exclusion has given way to a new one. In the old system, African-Americans were kept out of some areas and concentrated in others. Public housing was the vehicle. The new system is more insidious. Very poor African-Americans are removed from their homes in gentrifying areas and given a housing voucher to find housing that for

the most part doesn't exist. In our present ideological climate, where it is believed that success or failure can only be achieved through individual effort, the unsuccessful are easily demonized, dismissed, or evicted. Therefore, it is ironic that in the case of Cabrini-Green, the Gautreaux decision is being cynically used to block a redevelopment plan in which the development's tenants had a real voice. Instead, Gautreaux is being used to promote a new form of racial exclusion posing as a benign "mixed income" development policy. (*The Talking Drum*, no. 4 [2000])

This is not the place to discuss the Chicago Housing Authority's plan to demolish public housing or to survey what is now a nationwide movement to save public housing and fight the relocation of poor people and the gentrification of their neighborhoods. I merely wish to suggest that black people have had a lot to say about their problems and their communities' future—a lot that would directly challenge what Fiss assumes to be true.

Lastly, I would like to comment briefly on James Baldwin's curious role in Fiss's narrative. Baldwin appears throughout the text as a silent interlocutor, called into service to exemplify the experiences of black people and lend authority to Fiss's account of ghetto life—first as an example of those who fled "the confines of the ghetto" for "upscale neighborhoods" and later to embody the black church's failure at parenting. Needless to say, it was not the confines of the ghetto that led Baldwin into exile in Paris; it was the confines of American racism. Moreover, it was James Baldwin who coined the slogan "Urban Renewal Is Negro Removal" in response to an earlier scheme to depopulate "the ghetto." If Baldwin could speak, I suspect he would have a lot to say about this plan and about black poverty in contemporary America. And I suspect he would disagree with Fiss.

PART III

A TASK UNFINISHED

OWEN FISS

▓ Scarred by slavery, this nation has struggled with the issue of racial justice ever since its founding. The Civil War was a turning point, but even those who emerged victorious from that calamitous experience knew full well that true equality could not be achieved by simply declaring an end to slavery. Without a bold program of reconstruction, the vestiges of that institution would live on and a new caste structure would emerge, making a mockery of freedom.

The arduous process of reconstruction began in the years immediately following the Civil War. By 1875 that effort had collapsed, and by the end of the nineteenth century the nation had embarked on a very different course, embracing a state-supported system of separation, exclusion, and disenfranchisement known as Jim Crow. Soon enough, Jim Crow became a way of life and turned the former slaves and their children into second-class citizens.

Throughout the first half of the twentieth century, we were frequently reminded of how far we had departed from our constitutional commitment to equality. Then, on that fateful day in 1954, the High Court issued an edict condemning Jim Crow and called on us to begin once again the process of reconstruction. Many resisted this second attempt at reconstruction. Some even took up arms. Yet through the determined but diplomatic use of judicial power, the support of the coordinate branches of the federal government, and the mobilization of multitudes of citizens, largely spearheaded by Martin Luther King Jr., the most blatant forces of resistance were overcome.

The Second Reconstruction—as the period begun by *Brown v. Board of Education* is known—has come to an end, if not in the mid-1970s, then certainly in August 1996, when Congress enacted and President Clinton signed into law the welfare reform bill. That measure reinforced the jurisprudence of the Burger and Rehnquist Courts, and redefined the relationship of the federal government to the nation's poor, a disproportionate number of whom are black. The 1996 law denied that welfare is an entitlement and greatly enhanced the discretion of the states in administering the program. A noble chapter of American history was thereby closed.

It thus seems a propitious moment to reflect on the achievements of the Second Reconstruction and to define the challenges we face in the years ahead. Though we must, of course, remain ever vigilant against the continuation and resurgence of Jim Crow–type discrimination, and press for the full enforcement of 1960s civil rights laws, we must also recognize that the issues of racial justice have changed, in some cases as a result of these laws, and fashion the agenda of the much-needed Third Reconstruction accordingly.

At the time of *Brown*, America's caste structure had a decidedly racial character. Most blacks were poor, and, although their poverty posed significant obstacles to their upward mobility, their subjugation was principally racial—first, because racial discrimination acted as an independent constraint on their lives and, second, because the enormous economic disadvantages blacks suffered could be traced directly to their race.

Today, however, the hierarchical structure initially engendered by slavery and perpetuated by Jim Crow can no longer be characterized simply in terms of race. The situation of blacks as a class has improved significantly. According to the 2000 census, 32.3 percent of all black families have incomes of $50,000 or higher. (The median income for all American families is $50,891.) Blacks are graduating from the nation's most prestigious universities and are entering the professions in meaningful numbers. They participate in almost all walks of American life, and some hold the most public positions in the nation. As a consequence, the most disadvantaged group is not blacks in general but the black underclass, a sector of the black community defined by both race and class and which now shoulders the legacy of centuries of racial oppression.

To see the black underclass, as I do, as a manifestation of the caste structure set in motion by slavery and continued by Jim Crow, is not only to acknowledge the utterly deplorable conditions that individual members of this group must endure but also to underscore the structural constraints on their upward mobility—constraints imposed by an accumulation of social practices for which we as a nation are collectively responsible. As a result, we should see this form of stratification as an affront to the egalitarian ideals that animated our earlier efforts at reconstruction and that so define this nation. It represents a moral and constitutional betrayal that demands swift and effective remedial action, not only as a matter of sound public policy but as a requirement of justice.

THE SOURCES OF INEQUALITY

All the participants in the debate taking place in this volume acknowledge, in one way or another, the conflict between our egalitarian ideals and the maintenance of the black underclass. Differences arise over the remedy. In recent decades a host of in-place remedies have gained favor in political circles—enterprise zones, neo-WPA programs, charter schools, and new crime control strategies. These measures leave the ghetto intact and aim to improve the conditions of life within it. But because such conditions are inextricably tied to the social dynamics of the ghetto, these remedies have very little prospect of success. The ghetto is not just a neighborhood that happens to be poor and black; rather, it is a social structure that, by isolating and concentrating the worst off and separating them from jobs, helped to create the black underclass and threatens to perpetuate it across generations.

One respondent, James Rosenbaum, provides compelling evidence of the relationship between the underclass and the ghetto. Basing his argument on studies of the *Gautreaux* program, Rosenbaum points to improvements—he describes them as "amazing"—in the lives of ghetto residents of Chicago who were given an opportunity to move to better neighborhoods. As he concludes, "Housing policy can do more than provide shelter—it can radically improve people's lives." To this I add that, even more than radically improving lives, housing policy aimed at deconcentration can, if adopted on a broad enough scale, help to eradicate caste, and thus deepen and extend the process of reconstruction begun more than a century ago.

Stephen Gregory takes a more benign attitude toward life in the ghetto and claims that my proposal, and the *Gautreaux* remedy on which it is based, "ignores the ways that the black poor *themselves* have defined the problems facing their communities." This is, of course, not true. *Gautreaux* was born of the civil rights struggles of Chicago, and it expressed the hopes and desires of the black community there who sought for themselves and their children a better life than any could hope for living in the Robert Taylor Homes and other segregated public housing projects. They wanted what the more economically privileged among them—the so-called black middle class—had obtained for themselves: an opportunity to move to neighborhoods that were safer, more accessible to work, and served by better schools. The actions of the thousands of black families who applied for the *Gautreaux* vouchers and, later, the vouchers offered by the Moving to Opportunity program, expressed their own understanding of the problems their communities face as well as what could be done to guard against these difficulties.

Professor Gregory quotes at length from a newsletter of a citizen group—the Coalition to Protect Public Housing—that criticizes the way *Gautreaux* has been implemented. According to the newsletter, "Very poor African Americans are removed from their homes in gentrifying areas and given a housing voucher to find housing that for the most part doesn't exist." It would be most unfortunate if this were true, but it is very far from the program I contemplate or what the *Gautreaux* decision promised. To fulfill their purpose, of course, vouchers must be generous enough to enable their recipients to secure adequate housing. Efforts might even be needed to ensure that the supply of affordable housing in the receiving neighborhoods is sufficient. Nor would poor blacks, as the newsletter charges, be "removed from their homes." They would be offered the means to move if they chose to do so; their freedom would be enlarged.

Admittedly, if enough families exercise this choice and decide to move, others may feel the pressure to do the same. Buildings may become vacant, and private developers or public authorities may redevelop the area where the ghetto once stood. However, plans for redevelopment should require the provision of affordable housing for those who choose to remain; the absence of such a requirement would be a failure of the redevelopment plans, not of *Gautreaux* or the deconcentration program I propose. Any reform carries the risk of setting in motion a process of change that might turn out badly. The appropriate response to such a possibility is not to turn one's back on reform altogether and continue to suffer the consequences of the status quo; rather, it is to institute measures that prevent adverse contingencies from ever materializing.

Jennifer Hochschild understands the importance of reform. She, too, sees the ghetto as an institution that helped to create and maintain the underclass, and she supports the idea of providing those trapped within the ghetto with the resources they need to move to a better neighborhood. She qualifies her endorsement of deconcentration, however, and recommends cutting in half the amount allocated for relocation and using the remainder to improve life within the ghetto or to provide transportation systems that would give ghetto residents access to jobs in the suburbs. The appeal of such a proposal, designed to cover all bases, is obvious. Yet I fear that if we so limit deconcentration by cutting the available funds in half, the lives of those who remain trapped in the ghetto would be made even more miserable—for example, those who remain on the waiting list because there are not enough funds to go around.

To appreciate the downside of Hochschild's recommendation, we must remember that today's ghetto is not just a product of the containment policies of Jim Crow; its character also derives from the fact that, in recent decades, many of those most able to move out have already left. Although this exodus improved the life chances of these individuals, it also enhanced the concentration and isolation of the most disadvantaged. Richard Ford rightly points out that my proposal might intensify this very dynamic of isolation. As he explains, some of the most disadvantaged may refuse the subsidy offered and remain isolated in the ghetto, thereby creating what Ford calls a "super-underclass." I see no way of eliminating altogether the danger Ford describes by providing information to enable residents to weigh adequately the advantages of a move, but I believe it can be minimized. I fear that the qualifications Hochschild suggests would magnify considerably the risk of creating the so-called super-underclass. Limiting the subsidy, as she proposes, would prevent many who may want to move from doing so.

Robert Coles embraces the aspirations underlying integration but alerts us to the dysfunctions of the communities ghetto residents might move into and to the problems that might arise in the communities formed where the ghetto once stood. At the close of his essay he relates the comments of a father of four in Roxbury, Massachusetts, who contemplates the arrival of well-to-do white families in his neighborhood: "They're all dressed up and they are always trying to be fancy, and it's antique this, and antique that, and I worry that they are not inter-

ested in families—they are interested in *themselves*, in showing
themselves off. That is not what I want my kids to see."

In the end this father resolves to stand firm. He will not
"cut and run" but will remain in the community and shelter his
children from the newcomers' way of life. This man's worries
and determination to resist the influences on his children that
he finds so distasteful cannot but move us. Yet his concerns
should not be turned into a dictate of policy, much less of justice. To do so would require that we ignore the dangers those
trapped in inner-city ghettos face—a scarcity of jobs, poor
schools, street gangs, and high levels of crime. No parent wants
his or her children subjected to these threatening conditions,
but few can shelter their children from them.

Similarly Tracey Meares acknowledges the logic behind deconcentration but expresses a concern for the difficulties that
may be lurking in the new neighborhoods of those who choose
to move. Drawing on her own life experience, she poignantly
reminds us of the acts of discrimination that will cause pain to
those who move. Of course, her worry is well founded, but the
risk of such hardships is not a sufficient reason for rejecting the
deconcentration program I propose, for they do not outweigh
the hardships that ghetto residents suffer today. The dangers
that concern Tracey Meares exist in every form of integration,
including that mandated by *Brown v. Board of Education*. They
must not be a counsel of inaction, however; rather, as Gary
Orfield stresses in his contribution to this debate, they should
serve as a challenge to build new institutions in the receiving
communities to counter the risk of discrimination. I read Tracey Meares's expression of caution in a similar spirit.

Jim Sleeper's concern is of another character altogether. He
worries that those who might take advantage of the subsidy

may not actually be ready to move. He writes: "We should encourage and protect inner-city residents who want to move, provided they are more or less ready." However, he does not provide a mechanism for separating out those who are ready to move from those who are not; instead, he uses this idea of preparedness as a basis for favoring in-place strategies. "It would be far better," Sleeper insists, "to improve public transit and the educational and social preparation without which few moves to the suburbs are sustainable."

Such a view slights the empirical evidence marshaled by research in this area, including studies of the *Gautreaux* program in Chicago and the Moving to Opportunity program in Boston. These studies indicate dramatic improvements in the lives of those who moved, which suggests that those who live in the ghetto are far more prepared to move than Sleeper would have us believe. Sleeper's position also embodies a cruel irony: He knows that the preparation he calls for will come largely from holding a steady job, yet he also understands the dynamics that make jobs in the inner city scarce. He gives us no more reason than William Wilson does to believe that we could create jobs in the inner cities in sufficient number or quality to end the problems of joblessness that now pervade those communities.

Ultimately Sleeper turns from work as a training ground for life's challenges and puts his trust in what he calls "the readying potential of new and old inner-city education models, from Catholic to charter schools." Although those institutions, as well as public schools and Head Start, offer much to admire, they hardly seem able to sustain the enormous burden Sleeper would place on them, much less reverse the underlying dynamics responsible for the creation and perpetuation of the black underclass.

THE POSSIBILITY OF REFORM

Some of the responses to the deconcentration program I propose move the debate from justice to politics. Phillip Thompson, for instance, rejects deconcentration on the ground that it
will not be acceptable to what he calls "white suburbia"; instead,
he throws his support behind Wilson's in-place proposal because it is "a lot more politically realistic." Jim Sleeper, too,
chides me for failing to appreciate the complex "dynamics of
real estate, race, and politics" that animated the migration of
ethnic, working-class whites to the suburbs and turned the
communities that emerged into bastions of resistance. Speaking
more generally, I must confess that I was struck by the spirit of
defeatism that pervades the responses. Many of my interlocu-
tors hesitate to embrace deconcentration in all its fullness because they fear it is not politically feasible.

Buckminster Fuller once said that it is a virtue to be naïve.
Such a disposition preserves the sovereignty of justice and helps
to ensure that our judgment of what is just is not compromised
by our estimates of what is politically feasible. I, too, believe it
is a virtue to be naïve; but because we wish to make the world
just, not simply to understand justice, I also believe that there
is some virtue to realism. Although my purpose is to describe
what justice requires, I am mindful of the need to attend to the
forces that resist the delivery of justice, regardless of whether
they arise from incompetence, from a narrow regard for self-
interest, or from a difference of opinion about the requirements
of justice. We need to take account of the mood of Congress,
the interests served by containment, and the hostility that inte-

gration of the type I propose is likely to engender in the so-called receiving communities.

In the heated battles of politics, sometimes self-interest can be put to the service of justice, as we learned in the Second Reconstruction. Throughout the debates surrounding the Civil Rights Act of 1964, the advocates of reform often explained how opening public accommodations and jobs to blacks would be good for business. The eventual passage of that law could be seen as a triumph of both justice and economic interest. A similar dynamic may have been at work in the 1996 appropriations act for HUD.

That act required local public housing authorities to make viability assessments of their older, and what the act refers to as "distressed," projects by comparing the cost of revitalization to the cost of providing all the tenants with Section 8 vouchers. As a consequence, some of the worst public housing projects in the nation have been closed, and many tenants have been given a chance to move to a better neighborhood or to return to the same sites where the projects once stood, now rebuilt as mixed-income neighborhoods with varied forms of housing. The statute commanded that the tenants living in the projects being torn down be enabled to move to "decent, safe, sanitary, and affordable housing which is, to the maximum extent practicable, housing of their choice." Some defended the measure in purely economic terms, arguing that it makes no sense to throw good money after bad, yet we can see how justice was also served.

Extending the deconcentration program implicit in the 1996 act beyond the confines of public housing, as I urge, would not only serve justice but also would further important economic interests. Urban centers would be revitalized, and the human potential latent in the underclass would be liberated for more productive purposes. In estimating the feasibility of a civil rights remedy, we should not ignore the possibility of serving justice through the advancement of economic interests.

We must also be careful not to exaggerate, in the name of realism, the forces of resistance or the barriers to implementation, which, after all, vary from city to city—and sometimes from moment to moment. Alexander Polikoff, a long-time veteran of civil rights struggles and the lawyer who launched *Gautreaux* and successfully defended the sweeping deconcentration remedy before the Burger Court, wisely reminds us that "possibilities for moving toward justice may come at unlikely times."

To achieve justice in our own day we must focus on the pockets of goodwill that exist in this great nation, and nourish and develop them to the utmost. We must uncover the ghetto's social dynamic and explain how it creates and perpetuates the black underclass. Scientific studies of the impact of the *Gautreaux* plan and the more recent Moving to Opportunity program only confirm what common sense tells us, and will help to remove the vestiges of doubt about the ramifications of segregation and to strengthen the appeal of giving people a chance to leave the ghetto. These are the lessons that we should teach in the nation's classrooms today.

Polikoff warns of the "extreme fragility" of the sentiment of justice. My impression is just the opposite. One of the most distinctive features of American politics is how responsive power is to justice. Although resistance is sometimes fierce, we should not view the opponents of reform as intractable. Admittedly housing integration has always been intensely difficult. Even after the Civil Rights Act of 1964 opened the doors of public accommodations to blacks and helped to equalize employment opportunities in the private sector, Congress was slow to enact a fair housing law. Ultimately, however, Congress came to its senses and did what simple justice required. Although the fair housing law was passed after the assassination of Martin Luther King Jr. and a week of riots in more than a hundred cities throughout the nation, those events only accelerated the process of adopting a measure the enactment of which had been assured a month before, when the Senate voted to end a Southern filibuster.

Residents of upscale neighborhoods, whether they are white or black, may well try to fence out poor blacks arriving from the ghetto. Some may fear a diminution of property values or, as Sleeper emphasizes, the reemergence of the very problems they sought to avoid by moving to a better neighborhood. We must reckon with these concerns but not capitulate to them. We must choose the receiving communities carefully and, as Gary Orfield wisely counsels, support the changes that inevitably will occur in them. We must not only set changes in motion but also shepherd communities through these changes. We must not create new ghettos.

Our purposes must be clear. Deconcentration is not intended to secure for ghetto residents the right to choose one's residence, which would only pit the associational liberty of one group against that of another, but rather derives from the desire to eliminate a horrible inequality. In attempting to tear down the walls of the ghetto, we are trying to dismantle an institution that continues, in a different and more calibrated form, the caste structure that has disfigured our nation from the very beginning. "We must come to see," King once said, after the long march from Selma to Montgomery, "that the end we seek is a society at peace with itself, a society that can live with its conscience."

NOTES ON THE CONTRIBUTORS

AUTHORS

ROBERT COLES is a child psychiatrist and James Agee Professor of Social Ethics at Harvard University.

OWEN FISS is Sterling Professor of law at Yale University. He gratefully acknowledges the contributions to his work in this volume by John Bronsteen, Matthew J. Lindsay, William B. Michael, and Brandon L. Paradise.

RICHARD FORD is professor of law at Stanford University.

STEVEN GREGORY is director of Columbia University's Institute for Research in African-American Studies and is the author of *Black Corona: Race and the Politics of Place in an Urban Community* (Princeton University Press, 1998).

JENNIFER HOCHSCHILD is professor of government and Afro-American studies at Harvard University and is the author of *Facing Up to the American Dream: Race, Class, and the Soul of the Nation* (Princeton University Press, 1996).

TRACEY L. MEARES is professor of law at the University of Chicago Law School.

GARY ORFIELD is professor of education and social policy at Harvard University and codirector of Harvard University's Civil Rights Project.

ALEXANDER POLIKOFF is senior staff counsel with Business and Professional People for the Public Interest, and served as the lead counsel in the *Gautreaux* case.

JAMES E. ROSENBAUM is professor of sociology, education, and social policy at Northwestern University.

J. PHILLIP THOMPSON is associate professor of political science at Columbia University.

JIM SLEEPER is the author of *Liberal Racism* (New York: Penguin, 1998) and *The Closest of Strangers* (New York: Norton, 1991). He was the urban political columnist for the *New York Daily News* from 1993 to 1996. He is currently writing a book on American national identity.

EDITORS

JOSHUA COHEN is professor of philosophy and Sloan Professor of political science at the Massachusetts Institute of Technology. He is editor-in-chief of *Boston Review* and the author of numerous books and articles on political theory.

JEFFERSON DECKER is a former managing editor of *Boston Review.*

JOEL ROGERS is professor of law, political science, and sociology at the University of Wisconsin, a member of *Boston Review*'s editorial board, and author of numerous articles and books on American politics.

INDEX